Using Psychometrics in Coaching:
A Practical Guide

Using Psychometrics in Coaching: A Practical Guide

Ian Florance

Open University Press

Open University Press
McGraw Hill
8th Floor, 338 Euston Road
London
England
NW1 3BH

email: enquiries@openup.co.uk
world wide web: www.openup.co.uk

First edition published 2022

Copyright © Open International Publishing Limited, 2022

All rights reserved. Except for the quotation of short passages for the purposes of criticism and review, no part of this publication may be reproduced, stored in a retrieval system, or transmitted, in any form or by any means, electronic, mechanical, photocopying, recording or otherwise, without the prior written permission of the publisher or a licence from the Copyright Licensing Agency Limited. Details of such licences (for reprographic reproduction) may be obtained from the Copyright Licensing Agency Ltd of Saffron House, 6–10 Kirby Street, London EC1N 8TS.

Executive Editor: Eleanor Christie
Editorial Assistant: Zoe Osman
Content Product Manager: Alison Davis

A catalogue record of this book is available from the British Library

ISBN-13: 9780335248872
ISBN-10: 033524887X
eISBN: 9780335248889

Library of Congress Cataloging-in-Publication Data
CIP data applied for

Typeset by Transforma Pvt. Ltd., Chennai, India

Fictitious names of companies, products, people, characters and/or data that may be used herein (in case studies or in examples) are not intended to represent any real individual, company, product or event.

Praise page

"This classic stands alongside Rogers, Kline, and Ibarra as an essential foundation for every coach's bookshelf. Written with wisdom and empathy entirely from the coach's perspective – but by someone who has for decades also been one of the key figures in psychometric testing across Europe, it is the best of both worlds. Deep but clear explanations, vivid case studies, occasional laugh-out-loud humour, and relentlessly practical throughout, it has every single thing you need – and a few you didn't know you'd missed, from 'hilly profiles' to the secret history of Wonder Woman. Serious, comprehensive, warm and wise – strongly recommended."

Anne Scoular, Meyler Campbell

"This book is an enormously practical and user-friendly guide to using psychometric assessment in coaching. It steps away from more traditional approaches and uses of psychometrics to articulate in a straightforward, but certainly not simplistic way, how a coach might use a range of assessments in their 'everyday' coaching, for the clear benefit of the client. It is packed with interesting coaching examples, guidance and thought provoking information which is hugely relevant to all coaches and coaching psychologists, whatever their experience of coaching and approach may be. I recommend it very highly as a book you'll want to buy and consult on a regular basis."

Mary Watts, Emeritus Professor of Psychology,
City, University of London, UK

"This is the go-to book for coaches who want to properly assess their clients. It has all a coach needs to know to understand how assessments could be useful, and why they could be a waste of time! The chapters flow very well from setting the scene, to opening up the wider range of possible assessments available. There should be no excuse for a coach to simply use a single tool from the limited number of 'usual suspects' or dabble in the dubious array of uncertified internet offerings. Ian Florance has a great style, cutting through scientific jargon and marketing spin to make testing and assessment accessible for coaches. Stories from his career in this area, and multiple case studies bring out an authentic message."

Nigel Evans CPsychol, Director NEC & Chair of the
European Board of Assessment (EFPA)

"Ian Florance brings his years of knowledge as a publisher of psychometric assessments to his gift for coaching with the integrity that those familiar with his writing have come to expect. This exploration of the pros and cons and ways of using such assessments to further the quality of coaching for coaches and clients is seasoned with caution and wisdom such that my own initial scepticism about their use has given way to increased curiosity. That quality makes this book, in my view, a useful addition to the formation of any psychologically informed coach."

Alison Clarke, Coaching Psychologist, Chair Practice Board, British Psychological Society

Contents

List of Figures   ix

Acknowledgements   x

Introduction   xi
    Who is this book for?   xii
    What this book is not   xiii
    Case studies and assessment examples   xiii
    Tests, assessments and psychometrics   xiv

1. WHERE DO ASSESSMENTS HELP OR HINDER COACHING?   1

    Where assessment can contribute to coaching   2
    Where assessments can damage the coaching process and relationship   9
    Assessment in coaching: for or against?   14

2. USING ASSESSMENTS IN COACHING   15

    When to use assessments   15
    What to ask   18
    Responding to questions and comments coachees might make   20
    Preparing to administer and administering assessments   21
    Assessment feedback   25
    Research   25

3. ACCESSING THE RIGHT ASSESSMENTS   27

    Choosing assessments   30
    Training in assessment   34

4. THE RANGE OF ASSESSMENTS   37

    Types of test most coaches cannot use   37
    Tests and assessments   38
    Do coaches ever use tests?   41
    Tests and assessments: a conclusion   43
    A definition   43

5. ASSESSING PERSONALITY   44

    What is personality?   44
    Type measures   46
    Trait measures   54
    Ipsative measures   66

Projective measures 71
Summary 72

6. ASSESSING OTHER CHARACTERISTICS 74

Emotional intelligence 74
Other intelligences 78
Strengths 78
Motivation, values, resilience and stress 80
Interests, learning styles and trainability 87
Conflict 89
Repertory Grid Technique 90
Team roles 91
FIRO-B® 94
360s 95

7. 'IS THIS ASSESSMENT ANY GOOD?' WHAT THE TECHNICAL TERMS AND NUMBERS MEAN 98

What does this assessment claim to be measuring? 101
Does the assessment measure consistently and accurately? . . 103
To what extent can I rely on the scores? 104
Does it provide rich information in an economical way? 105
Is an assessment fair? 105
What is an acceptable correlation? 106
Summary 106

8. THE FUTURE 107

Aspects of assessment that don't change or change less 107
New sources of information 108
Transforming test items 109

9. CONCLUSION 111

Glossary 113
Bibliography 116
Index 119

List of figures

Figure 4.1: Types of ability test item	39
Figure 4.2: Structure of human abilities	39
Figure 4.3: Types of assessment item	41
Figure 5.1: Some types of personality assessment	46
Figure 5.2: The normal curve of distribution	50
Figure 5.3: Bimodal distribution	51
Figure 5.4: Profile produced by an imaginary trait-based personality test	57
Figure 5.5: An item format for rating	67
Figure 5.6: An item format for ranking	67
Figure 5.7: A forced choice assessment item	68
Figure 5.8: Different approaches to assessing personality	73
Figure 6.1: Motives, values, strengths and resilience	80
Figure 6.2: My version of the Thomas–Kilmann styles of handling conflict	89
Figure 6.3: Underlying thinking of FIRO-B®	94
Figure 9.1: An assessment starter pack for coaches	112

Acknowledgements

Anne Scoular opened the door to the world of coaching for me. Her colleagues at Meyler Campbell, particularly Catherine Devitt and the late Juan Coto, helped me understand what coaching offers and demands. Professor Mary Watts invited me to work on a number of coaching projects, commented on this manuscript and is an unfailingly supportive colleague. Dave Stent contributed experiences and case studies, drawing on his long career in and unmatched knowledge of coaching.

Among many others, Professor John Rust, Nigel Evans, Suchi Pathak and past and present members of the European Test Publishers Group have taught me much of what I know about assessment.

Eleanor Christie, Zoe Osman and others at McGraw-Hill Education/Open University Press have been unfailingly efficient, encouraging and perceptive at a time when publishers are under huge pressure. Thank you!

Jenny Rogers made this book happen. She suggested it, sharpened the outline and has made hundreds of improvements to the text. She has contributed her in-depth experience of coaching and testing with great generosity and added insights throughout.

But I am solely responsible for the views I express and consequent errors.

Myers-Briggs Type Indicator®, Myers-Briggs®, MBTI® and MBTI Step II® are trademarks or registered trademarks of Myers & Briggs Foundation, Inc. in the United States, and other countries. FIRO®, FIRO-B® and TKI® are trademarks or registered trademarks of The Myers-Briggs Company in the United States and other countries.

16pf® is a registered trademark of the Institute for Personality & Ability Testing, Inc.

Introduction

Why should coaches use assessments? Coach training introduces a huge variety of techniques so why bother with another one which might seem, at first glance, over-technical?

This book argues that more formal assessments can make your coaching relationships more effective by introducing a third, informed, objective voice into your conversations. High-quality assessment reports can help overcome blocks, create A-HA moments and encourage rich disagreement. This book provides a guide to the world of assessment: what type of assessments are available; what they address; how to choose what you will use; identifying and training in your preferred tools; where and when to use them in coaching; and some of the developments you can expect to see now and in the future. I have sketched how assessment developed; why there has been a stand-off between it and coaching; and why the language of assessment can seem unhelpful to coaches. Theoretical background should illuminate practical issues rather than get in their way. Having read the book, you should possess the basic tools and vocabulary to explore in more depth the world of assessment, which can seem initially off-putting, and get the best out of it.

Only you can decide if assessments will be useful to you, considering the areas in which you coach, the types of clients you work with and your own unique approach to the coaching relationship. This book can help you make an informed decision and, if you would find them useful, choose the right techniques.

If coaching is 'a pragmatic trade drawing on borrowed theory' (Rogers 2016: 6), assessment has not displayed such practical characteristics in the past and that's why the relationship between coaching and psychometric assessment has sometimes resembled, if not a war, at least a slightly nervous treaty negotiation. But both areas have changed dramatically in the last 30 to 40 years. Revolutions in technology and wider societal factors are bringing them closer together. That increasing proximity should make this book particularly timely.

I focus on the relevance of assessment to coaching, rather than offering another more general treatment of the use of assessment in a wider range of applications, the minute detail of how it works or theoretical debates about its efficacy. I've found that adopting a coaching viewpoint has generated unexpected conclusions, different from those of other books on the subject.

Testing and assessment initially focused on research into people as scientific subjects and the creation of accurate measurement to allow experts to categorise people or make difficult decisions about them. Testing involved (and in many cases still involves) experts with specialist knowledge making decisions about others. This approach runs directly counter to the emphasis in coaching on relationships, discussion and power balance. If psychometrics has traditionally seen itself as a numerical science, coaching developed as a humanistic practice.

I argue that, in coaching, accuracy of measurement is less important than the quality of assessment reports and the ability of the latter to engage coachees and stimulate conversation. Measurement excellence is still important but a less accurate assessment creating an appropriate report using insightful language will be more use in coaching than an accurate assessment with a report that resembles the small print of an insurance policy. Assessment reports which fit how coaching is done offer one more voice in a conversation, not a journal paper or a jury verdict. Any hint that the person taking an assessment is 'data in a scientific experiment' runs counter to the underlying philosophy of coaching.

Many assumptions that were originally made about the types of issues that assessment is designed to measure seem just that: assumptions. Some of them – for instance about the stability of personality and whether emotional intelligence can be taught, given what sort of thing it might be – are seemingly contradicted by the successful changes achieved through coaching, counselling, development and training. Put loosely: if some aspects of people don't change, why do governments, companies and partners spend lots of time and mountains of money trying to change them?

Because of these issues, many coaches prefer to use assessments which may have technical measurement flaws but which genuinely stimulate talk. But assessment and coaching are not on either side of a buffer zone sniping at each other. I will show that more assessments are appearing which genuinely contribute to successful coaching.

For all these reasons, some seeming assessment issues emphasised by writers from other backgrounds are not problems for coaches at all. But there is still some way to go.

Who is this book for?

This book is for people who are interested in coaching, considering training or already training in the area, or who are practising coaches aiming to develop their skills further. Your training may have covered one or two assessments and you want to learn about more. Perhaps a client has asked you to use an assessment with which you are not familiar or you have never thought that assessment had a place in your practice.

Coaches may work as external suppliers to profit-driven and not-for-profit organisations while employed managers and leaders may take a coaching approach to their role. Coaches work with sports teams, children in schools, offenders in prisons and with many different people on topics often labelled as 'lifestyle issues'. Other applications have emerged and are still emerging: trauma and mental health are examples. Assessment can play different roles and presents slightly different problems and possibilities in each of these areas. Where they seem relevant, I have noted these differences but much of the book applies across the full spectrum of coaching since it gives information which, combined with your particular experience and knowledge, will help you make decisions.

What this book is not

This is not an academic work, nor is it a piece of research. While I've referenced quotations where necessary, I have tried to avoid the style of 'death by a thousand brackets' which makes many academic titles unreadable to us ordinary mortals. On the other hand, I've referred to books and other sources which will help you investigate these issues further; these are listed in the Bibliography at the end.

Reading it will not qualify you to buy and use assessments. But it should help you decide if, and then how, you train and in which assessments.

I have avoided most of the detailed statistics which comprise a large part of the agenda for certain sorts of assessment training – in particular, for those used in industrial selection or for clinical diagnosis – and which many prospective users find so off-putting. I have however discussed concepts, such as validity, standardised scores and reliability, which are expressed in numbers. Understanding what these concepts mean contributes to choosing the right assessment for the right purpose. Professionally designed and delivered assessment training will cover the detail of statistics.

Inaccurate assessments, where you cannot know what is being measured and therefore what the scores mean, can be found everywhere online. You can buy many of them without training. They can harm people's lives, careers and mental health as surely as untested medicines (or vaccines – a particularly important issue now) used by people with no medical qualifications can damage physical health. In order to use measurement, you do need to use a specialist body of knowledge but much of it is common sense, drawing on what people do every day.

Case studies and assessment examples

This book uses case studies and refers to and discusses specific assessments. The case studies are anonymised. Some report individual experiences from my own coaching practice; some conflate a number of instances. I've asked colleagues and friends to give examples and merged different stories.

I also reference and discuss specific assessments throughout the book, particularly in Chapters 4, 5 and 6. Testing and assessment publishing is a high churn business, so assessment and publisher references go out-of-date quickly. Nevertheless, descriptions of specific assessments are important to get an understanding of the area. I use these examples where they best demonstrate an issue, technical point, or approach. To do this, I've sometimes described an earlier version of an assessment which has now been updated. These examples also, at times, discuss the most widely used version of a type of assessment or identify different approaches from a dominant assessment. When I name a particular assessment, I am not recommending it. I have raised criticisms and suggested the benefits of certain titles, but this book should give you a sense of the range available, where you can get information about different titles and the types of questions to ask.

Tests, assessments and psychometrics

I use 'assessment' rather than 'test' as the default word to indicate the topic of this book.

Coaches tend to use assessments: psychological measuring techniques that demand answers which are neither objectively right nor wrong but look at typical, default, characteristics of an individual. Instruments denoted by the word 'test' or its derivatives measure knowledge of an area or your ability to work out the correct answers to a problem; they have right and wrong answers. These latter are used in school assessment, workplace recruitment and measurement of certain clinical conditions. I'll occasionally use the word 'test' or its derivatives when I'm talking about these sorts of techniques, but people often join 'testing and assessment' together to indicate the overall area this book covers. The glossary and Chapter 7 go into this issue in slightly more detail.

'Psychometrics' used in the title of this book, indicates the aspect of psychology which deals with the measurement of psychological characteristics. So, this book deals with tools that have grown out of the science of psychology rather than any other area (astrology for instance – though I have a few words about that).

Some years ago, I worked for the leading UK publisher of clinical, educational and occupational assessments. Having had no formal training in people management (or in much else apart from the Victorian novel and early modern sculpture), I was sent by my boss on a two-week course at Ashridge Management College. One of the lecturers was a psychologist and, as part of this strand of the course, the trainees took a number of assessments including the Myers-Briggs Type Indicator® (MBTI®) and a measure of Belbin® Team Roles. I soon found myself being paraded around the college as the first male director to attend the course to have my particular personality profile. The point of this story was that the assessment results led to a series of conversations with the tutor about styles of management. They were informal chats, not formal coaching, but they revolutionised how I managed and gave me more confidence to be myself at work. For the first time I realised that there was no one correct way to manage: there were different styles which had to stem from individual characteristics if they were to work effectively. Adapting your style was not only *not* wrong, it had a name ('situational management') and was seen by many people as a successful approach to getting the best out of people. My particular personality and interests, which had before this seemed somewhat too '1960s influenced' to work in a for-profit company, were no longer seen as a weakness needing treatment. The assessment results had triggered this insight.

More recently I undertook one of my regular interviews for *The Psychologist*, the British Psychological Society's magazine. The interviewee was Anne Scoular, founder of the coach training company Meyler Campbell. A while later, Anne asked me to attend the Meyler Campbell coaching course and, in our discussions, she suggested that learning to be a coach doesn't just give you new skills: 'You'll find it changes your life'. She was right. My tutor, Juan Coto, and the other people I met during my training, helped me understand the way I viewed other people, how I expressed myself and the questions I asked. In particular, it altered how I listened to people in everyday life and, I believe and hope, made me shut up occasionally. It also taught me the danger of continually acquiescing and the strength of sympathetic but firm challenging of others.

Both assessment and coaching have provided those moments of personal discovery which, on the occasions they occur, are among the most memorable events in our lives and the most thrilling results of working in a coaching relationship. I have a foot in both camps: over 30 years working in every application of assessment from school tests to diagnostics of mental illness to developmental assessments; and five or six years (and counting) as a coach. This book is an attempt to negotiate a peace treaty between the two forces and get them working practically to improve coaching at a time when the need for it is growing.

1 Where do assessments help or hinder coaching?

To answer this question, it will help to look in more detail at why the two areas have previously missed each other. This will give context for both their increasing co-operation and continuing obstacles to it.

One of the assumptions behind coaching is that the people who are being coached already know the answers to the questions they're posing, often without realising the fact. Coach and client work together to 'surface' and acknowledge them, then create the conditions for the client to act.

Coaches do not necessarily need specialist, technical knowledge. For instance, you may or may not have psychology training or you might be a novice about the sector or role in which a coachee works. I've coached a number of executives in the automotive industry and my first confession was that I have never learnt to drive. Coaches should not need to share the religious and cultural background of their coachees though this point is increasingly questioned and researched. Specialist knowledge can at times lead to unhelpful dogmatism.

Successful coaches should 'be psychologically minded' as well as possessing a toolkit of techniques and models drawn from many different disciplines, experiences and theories. Coaches should also be receptive without being pushovers. Equality between coach and coachee is a precondition for coaching, not just a desired characteristic. Coaches use words and other information (for instance, body language) but may be suspicious of numbers unless they come from a more numbers-based background or are undertaking quantitative research. Coaching stresses the future.

Assessment and testing have looked different. Assessment has tended to be done **to**, rather than **with**, a person. Assessment administrators were, and often still are, psychologists, a profession which has defined much of the assessment enterprise since the late 19th century. Many psychologists used assessments to generate data which they interpreted using their professional knowledge and skills, telling the person who took the instrument, or a significant other such as a parent, something they didn't know, categorising or making decisions about them: 'This child is better at verbal reasoning than 90 per cent of the nine-year-olds you are teaching'; 'You suffer from mild aphasia'; 'Your ability levels suggest you should not aim to be a brain surgeon'; 'We can offer you this job'.

The model for this is hard science: controlling variables in order to identify or measure focused characteristics of the world (and universe) accurately. Thus, 'standardised' assessments were administered in laboratory-type environments. The assessment user was a type of experimental scientist dealing with data. The assessment subject was often precisely that. The outcomes of research were seen as universally applicable whatever the environment, as are the laws of physics if they are to be considered scientific laws at all.

At one time, training in these sorts of techniques emphasised that printed interpretations should never be shared with assessment takers for fear, among other issues, that they might misinterpret the highly specialist vocabulary in which these reports were written, even though the information in the reports was, precisely, a self-description. While all this has changed somewhat, there are still some areas (clinical testing, for instance, and what are known as 'high stakes decisions' such as deciding who should get a job), in different geographical areas, which treat assessment interpretations as more akin to pharmaceutical products – their use arbitrated by a specific professional group who 'prescribe' them to a sometimes uncomprehending 'patient'.

The 'fuel' of assessment is numbers. Its initial findings have to be translated into words. In many people's minds, the paradigms of testing are the tests/examinations they took at school (and which often haunted their middle-aged dreams at times of stress).

If the initial model of assessment was the hard science experiment, then coaching often sounds like a novelist talking to a character: the two parties learning from each other. No wonder the two areas have, at times, missed each other. Yet assessment and coaching have been moving closer together. A number of factors have influenced this.

In certain countries, for certain applications, non-psychologists now use assessments which once might have been reserved for psychologists. The creation of a competency framework and training courses to allow HR and other managers, consultants and coaches to use work-based assessments is one example but psychometric tools are also used in schools, doctors' surgeries and by non-psychologist therapists, such as those specialising in rehabilitation and speech and language therapy. A major growth area is the use of psychometric assessments in 'performance': elite and grass roots sports; music, acting and dance. I have even seen versions of psychometric assessments for sale from machines sited at metro stations in South Korea. This increased use partly stems from an increased understanding of how physical and psychological factors affect each other.

Economic factors have also increased their usage. The whole assessment process – from administration to writing the report – is overwhelmingly automated, using specifically created software, arguably reducing the need for once highly valued, specialist knowledge. This has widened the numbers and types of users, reducing total cost of some forms of testing and assessment.

Where assessment can contribute to coaching

In this section I use terms to describe the results and psychological make up of individuals; examples include 'conscientiousness' and 'introversion'. These are used to explain points and do not reflect the precise definitions used in particular assessments.

Understanding yourself and how your own psychology might impact your coaching practice and self-awareness

> Gertrujd was a successful lawyer but decided to change career and become a self-employed coach. She learnt about, completed and was given feedback on a number of assessments during training. She and her coach discussed the results.
>
> Her 'preference' was to act in a 'highly introvert' way. In ordinary conversation this might indicate she was shy, depressed or stand-offish. In this context, it suggested she needed less stimulation than some other people and expended a lot of energy being with other people, needing time alone to recharge. She tended to be quieter than the general UK population and thought more before she spoke. Her focus was on what was going on inside her rather than events in the outside world.
>
> Gertrujd scored high on 'agreeableness'. She put a high value on getting on with other people and was prepared to compromise her views in order to ensure harmony. On a measure of emotional intelligence, she seemed to emphasise understanding and controlling her own emotions but – and this surprised her – paid much less attention to what other people might be feeling. Conversations with friends and colleagues confirmed this finding. High in the rank order of her self-reported strengths were thinking before acting and ensuring that people worked well together. 'Putting herself in other people's shoes' was towards the bottom of her ranking.
>
> There were other results from such extensive assessment, but the ones listed above had most impact. They gave her and her course tutor a shared language to discuss issues and work out how they could shape her coaching practice. They agreed on actions to reflect these findings.
>
> Her 'introvert preference' suggested she would not have any difficulty with 'keeping her mouth shut and keeping her ears open', which is the major challenge for the majority of trainees. Coachees communicate in a variety of ways: from the language they use and tone of voice to their bodily posture. Gertrujd's internal focus meant she might miss out on some of this useful information. Also, she might not be able to reassure coachees that she was giving them full attention. Gertrujd practised concentrating on coachees and started using her wristwatch as a trigger to refocus if she found her attention wandering. The 'source of energy' issues suggested to Gertrujd that she should only ever undertake two coaching sessions in a day, with a reasonable gap in-between, a decision which had huge implications for the type of practice she set up, the clients she took on and what she billed per session.
>
> Her score on agreeableness suggested she might be prone to 'collusion': agreeing with the coachee to 'keep the peace'. It also suggested that Gertrujd might find difficulty in challenging coachees to surface the true reason for statements. Practising challenging in an appropriate way was a key, rewarding part of her training.

Raising the self-awareness of coachees

Most coaches who use assessments well attest to their power and, in particular, that of well-written reports, in raising coachees' self-awareness. Sometimes they offer welcome confirmation of what the self-aware individual already knows or suspects; sometimes they provide a pivotal moment. For instance, externally focused clients of mine have often missed the effect their behaviour has had on others or the way in which an external event has covertly affected their mental state. Realising their focus helped them to work on these issues.

Results can provide confirmation for insights achieved during coaching conversations or initiate conversations which lead to such insights.

Measuring progress

Effective coaching relationships result in an actionable goal: establishing one can take many sessions. It is critical to continue to discuss, finesse and investigate what a coachee genuinely wants to achieve until a goal has been agreed, rather than lose patience and jump to discussion of a fuzzy goal. Assessments should not be used in isolation to achieve this outcome. However, they can inform and shape the process, and show both coach and coachee what progress is being made both in shaping goals and putting them into action.

Aidan had moved into the role of International Director for a smaller, entrepreneur-run company, moving from a large corporation. Despite his experience, he was finding it exceedingly difficult to put his point of view across in board meetings. An initial administration of a measure of personality had confirmed his own view of himself. He tended to follow external rules; adhering to timescales and completing tasks set for him. It was important to him to have time to think through problems and issues, taking hard facts into account, before expressing an opinion. He was extremely uncomfortable if asked to react 'off-the-cuff'. His way of thinking and contributing clashed with an emotionally volatile CEO who demanded immediate responses. This was reducing Aidan's overall self-confidence.

We worked together and Aidan decided to implement a number of techniques for taking more control in board meetings. In order to make it clearer what he was trying to achieve (and whether he was achieving it), we agreed a number of techniques.

Aidan nominated five sympathetic colleagues. I constructed a simple informal questionnaire which asked them to rate Aidan's performance in meetings on certain criteria on a scale of one to five. He also answered a formal psychometric questionnaire which rated his preference for assertiveness against that of the general population as well as a group of international directors. The initiatives helped us establish goals. These involved, within three months: improving his assertiveness scores; moving the ratings by his colleagues an average of one point up; getting agreement in a board meeting for one major initiative against the initial resistance of his boss.

Aidan implemented the strategies we had agreed and soon started receiving informal feedback from other board members that suggested these were working. He felt happier with his performance. After three months he retook the second questionnaire, and I asked his colleagues to fill in the first one again. This enabled us to estimate any improvement, decide whether we needed to work further on the area, could work on some other issues or end the coaching engagement.

This process had benefits for both of us. Given Aidan's preference for facts and measures, the two questionnaires helped him, more than the informal comments by others, to accept that he was making progress. Partially defining the goals through test results enabled him to be able to see whether he had or had not achieved what he set out to do. That he had done this enthused him and motivated him to continue with the techniques past this initial period. The numbers also impressed the firm's HR manager, who had sponsored the coaching engagement. It gave her hard evidence that there was a return on her investment in coaching, enabling her in turn to justify it to a sceptical CEO.

Providing a shared language

The components which make up personality, known as dimensions or factors, are given names. You need to understand their definitions with clarity, and to use them correctly if you are going to use a particular assessment tool well. Where everyday words are used for this purpose, confusion over what is actually being reported becomes a danger: 'agreeableness' is an example; another is 'warmth'. In addition, different questionnaires use the same word to denote an area they are measuring, but each might define it in a different way: introversion is a common example of this.

Despite these confusing features, many reports are now written to encourage insight and discussion rather than to put off the uninitiated. I share reports with coachees, knowing that we will discuss them and can correct any misunderstandings stemming from specialist use of language. The reason I do this is partly to ensure coachees understand that I have no 'hidden knowledge' about them. If you say you work in coaching or psychology, some people will immediately comment: 'Ah, so you know why I'm doing this?' or 'Careful folks, we have a mind-reader here!' These responses are light-hearted but enshrine unhelpful beliefs. Sharing questionnaire outcomes appropriately corrects this sort of misunderstanding but can achieve more than that.

Many people find it more or less difficult to discuss psychological issues. In a work context they feel such an internal focus might indicate weakness or self-indulgence. In other contexts, it might be felt to be too self-revelatory. Underlying instances of this reluctance is the fact that some people do not have a specific vocabulary to discuss these topics, or a vocabulary which avoids sometimes unhelpful emotional reactions.

Contrary to this point, culture is becoming more psychologised, not least by the arts and entertainment. In particular, younger people seem more comfortable using psychological language. Tests and assessments actually help coach and coachee agree a language, thus overcoming any reluctance to start talking about psychological issues. Dave Stent, a coach with in-depth experience of assessment, believes that 'offering a shared vocabulary to overcome reluctance at the start of a coaching relationship, then to continue those discussions, is one of the main benefits of using questionnaires in coaching.'

A commonly understood language encourages genuine, substantive disagreement ('No, that's not what I mean'; 'No that does not reflect what I'm like') rather than disagreement over the meaning of the words being used.

When I give reports to coachees, I ask them to tick the statements they think are true and put crosses beside ones which they think are wrong, even grading how strongly they feel by putting in one to three ticks or crosses to show how much they agree or disagree. Our next sessions are often notably useful ones in which we focus on areas where coachees disagree with their reports. I ask them to give me instances of behaviour which prove the results to be wrong. This can lead to breakthroughs in self-understanding. For instance, the report on one leader I worked with suggested he had little empathy, acted without much forethought, was controlling, had limited verbal ability and high numerical ability, could never work alone and was rarely in control of his emotions. He felt this description was tantamount to libel and suggested, in clear anatomical terms, what I could do with it. But the following conversations centred around the detail of actual incidents, such as a major disagreement with a senior manager and the redundancy of a trainee salesperson. This led to substantial personal insight and concrete action.

Respectful disagreement generates breakthrough thinking. A shared language is essential for this.

Understanding the coaching relationship and individual differences

You don't have to like everyone to work effectively with different individuals, but you must understand and respect their differences.

The setting was a publishing company. Two specialists exhibited different work behaviours but needed to co-operate closely on a high-profile project with several hundred thousand pounds at risk. One of the employees was a commissioning editor: a person who worked with authors – in this case a well-known film star – to bring in a manuscript which would sell; also dealing with agents and many other parties within the company, to convince them of the characteristics and importance of the project.

The other person was the production editor whose job it was to sort out the manuscript, ensure it was well-written, correct, legally unassailable and consistent in its detail; to reflect the author's (sometimes exacting and specific) wants about text and illustration; to organise the typesetting and get it to the designer, typesetter and printer in time for sale in the critical pre-Christmas sales period. Miss that and the book would have to be delayed a year.

Because of their differences they caused problems on the project, as they had on others before. Their manager described their relationship as 'dysfunctional'. She called in an external coach to sort out the problem. Both people took a battery of psychometric tools. The results were perhaps not a surprise but externalised and made vivid what everyone in the company knew. The production editor might be described loosely as a conscientious, completer-finisher with high, internally driven quality standards which meant he only finished a project when he was happy with it while the views of other people counted for little. His convergent focus of attention meant he could only concentrate one thing at a time. This gave him a superb eye for detail when spotting errors in and correcting a manuscript. The commissioning editor could be described as highly extrovert and sociable, exploratory, flexible and spontaneous. She completed tasks to a quality level which 'got the job done' but was not worried about perfection for its own sake. In her view it was more desirable to get the outcomes of a project 90 per cent right and deliver them on time, rather than 100 per cent right two weeks late. She often failed to finish or even start jobs she had taken on but focused on what she considered to be most important, since they would have the most visible impact. She always took time to investigate new ideas. You can see how the former would think the latter a dangerously sloppy dilettante; the latter would see the former as a boring bureaucrat – an obstacle to be overcome.

The assessment results made it possible to help them understand where their behaviour genuinely harmed effective work and needed to change; how they might strike the other; where their strengths fitted into project process; what the other one contributed and where; how they could cross the borders of their jobs to improve the process they were involved in. The production editor understood that without the commissioning editor they would be inflexible and unable to innovate. The commissioning editor had a huge skill in handling often difficult, ego-driven authors and had to make compromises to get a manuscript at all. The commissioning editor began to understand that the production editor's approach was essential to avoid disaster. Work with them – both coaching and mentoring – enabled them to value the different approach of each other and see how it complemented their own.

There was no perfect Hollywood ending. They still disagreed at times. In fact, there have to be different points of view to get the best possible book to market: total agreement would have led to unacceptable as well as necessary compromises (another insight the assessment and resultant coaching highlighted for them).

What works with a two-person team operating a process can work for an eleven-person team, a six-person board or a family.

Just as this sort of understanding, facilitated by psychometrics, works in developing healthy team dynamics, it would help coach and coachee to understand how they can work together and what they could contribute to their coaching relationship.

Understanding what motivates change

Many coaches use models like GROW. This was developed in the 1980s by Graham Alexander, Alan Fine and Sir John Whitmore. GROW is an acronym for:

Goal
Reality
Options
Will

As the last letter emphasises, this model and others encourage discussion of the extent to which a coachee has the genuine will or desire to change. Discriminating between whether someone is in a position to change and whether someone actually wants to change is as important as, in a recruitment or promotion context, discriminating whether someone has the skills and ability to achieve success in an area and whether they actually want to do it. Coachee motivation is one of the keys to effective coaching

Getting this wrong can damage the coaching process and relationship. It was once pointed out to me that trying to motivate certain types of creative people through the promise of extra money or a bigger job title risked demotivating them! My experience in publishing proved this to be true. I once offered a pay rise to a Java programmer who worked for me. His response was: 'I don't need more pay. I get bored with the easy problems you give me. Put me on projects that give me headaches and I'll work as hard as you like.' This seemed too strange to be true, but experience confirmed it. Getting right what really motivates someone is key to helping coachees turn goals into actions: a formal assessment of motivation will reduce mistakes and misunderstandings.

Providing justification for coaching costs to sponsors

Is coaching worth the amount of money spent on it? Can you prove that it has been effective in achieving what it set out to do? Has there been a payback on the cost of a particular coaching programme: if so, how much? These questions have haunted certain coaching applications for some time. Groves and Furnham (2016) introduce the issues.

To draw on experience in an adjacent field, organisational recruitment has set out to provide measures of whether procedures deliver value-for-money. The search for returns on investment (ROIs) for testing in recruitment processes has developed sometimes complex, sometimes dubious, computations. These balance estimates of assessment costs against money saved by a more efficient recruitment/selection process and the effectiveness of candidates chosen using assessments as against those chosen without them. These latter use a variety of performance criteria ranging from managers' ratings to the order values a salesperson has won. None of these specific ROIs has been universally accepted and many look like a fudge. But you could imagine a similar equation to compute the effectiveness and value of a coaching programme. What was the expenditure on coaching as against the money saved or generated by the improved performance of coachees?

This might be too impressionistic to express in monetary terms and such an attempt may be irrelevant for non-organisational coaching purposes: it certainly runs counter to the prevailing philosophy of coaching in that it treats people as means rather than ends. However, questionnaires allow coaches to answer the question 'What effect has the coaching had on the psychological characteristics of the coachee?' with numbers rather than impressions. Reassessing someone on the same instrument at the end of a coaching programme may show how much progress has been made in specific targeted behaviours.

This issue of effectiveness is not just important to sponsors. Professional coaches need feedback on their effectiveness and also need to know when a coaching process has reached its goals.

Where assessments can damage the coaching process and relationship

On the basis of the above, you would wonder what the problem is; why have psychometric assessment and coaching been at loggerheads? If assessments are that useful to coaches, why don't they use hundreds of them with every candidate? I know a few people, newly qualified in an assessment, who seem to want to do exactly that. Here are some of the reasons why caution is needed.

Imposition of structure on the coaching relationship from the beginning

Coaching relationships are shaped by two core influences. The first is what coachees want, or find they want to talk about: the issues that are uppermost in their minds or which have been hidden and are surfaced during coaching. This emphasis is stressed in all high-quality coaching training. Coachees define the agenda from the beginning of the engagement and throughout each session.

The second influence is the coach's understanding of how coaching works and how this translates into techniques for keeping coaching 'on track'.

These two influences can work against each other, and part of the job of the coach is to keep them in balance. Being driven *entirely* by what coachees state as their agenda, without challenge or questioning, can lead to a loss of effectiveness. Trained coaches know that without this latter discipline, coaching can transform into a meandering series of more or less helpful conversations with no end point. This may prove useful for the coachee; as a colleague once commented, 'What's wrong with that if it helps?'. However, it isn't coaching and it is certainly not what the sponsor or payee thinks they're getting. Any experienced coach will hear alarm bells when they feel the sessions becoming cosy fireside chats with little or no challenge. Most particularly, it is the role of the coach in any engagement to help coachees articulate what they do want to work on and achieve. It can take some time and effort to do that.

Equally too much structure, defined by the coach, undermines the fundamentals of coaching – that coachees are resourceful and know what they want, and that power is equalised in the relationship. Questionnaire results can impose an external structure on coaching sessions which upsets this balance.

Comprehensive training courses will provide both guidance and practice in feeding back psychometric results from a particular instrument in a variety of situations from recruitment to careers guidance to development. Generalised assessment feedback will tend to emphasise one-way communication: making sure the subject has understood results. It is weighted towards training and mentoring models. When you learn different instruments, you'll discover different ways of structuring this feedback: 'look at extreme high or low scores'; 'search for these profiles'; 'use this scale to interpret others'; 'look for similarities/exceptions'. The structure of any psychometric assessment and its report can distort the structure of a coaching session if the coach is not careful. In doing this, it might negate the agenda of a coachee.

As an example, an assessment might suggest that someone has difficulty in contributing his or her views at any meeting at work. This might lead the coach to start developing strategies for improving communication. But the results might be indicating any one of a number of deeper issues. The coachee might have been bullied by their manager and simply be scared. I've often found problems outside work interfering with attention at work: tiredness, ill-health and lack of exercise affect performance, as does low self-esteem. And sometimes a coachee might be finding it difficult to admit that they are out of their depth, in the wrong job or a failed relationship. This is just a sample of the list of hypotheses a coach might develop and investigate. I used the word 'hypotheses' deliberately because the development and appropriate presentation of hypotheses is a critical skill that coaches use and one of the areas where assessment can help them.

Even well-used assessments can only offer signposts. They do not provide final destinations and may misrepresent the person completing them: no assessment is perfect. The resultant journey rests on coaching and the balance between the influences I outlined above. Used without thought, assessments can lead to premature goal setting and a misunderstanding of what the coachee actually thinks is going on and wants to do about it. They can impose their own structures on the way coaching is done and can cause coaches to focus on internal psychological factors and be blind to others, such as environmental influences.

Being the listener rather than the speaker is the first and often the most difficult area of coach training. Speaking seems to justify; listening looks like relaxation. Speaking is contributing which justifies payment; listening resembles opting out. Speaking seems active; listening seems passive. Instead of listening to the coachee vent for half an hour, assessment can impose a structure,

Where do assessments help or hinder coaching? **11**

allowing the coach to control the agenda and be actively involved in processes of administration, interpretation, feeding back and, sometimes, teaching. If the coach understands an assessment and the coachee does not, the coach is in control.

Masking coaching incompetence and reducing imposter syndrome

Preparing for this book I talked to two colleagues who had come to coaching with more testing knowledge than I have. In our conversations we agreed that our initial, post-training coaching sessions had a default stage: in this we suggested that the coachee took an assessment that we knew. We also agreed that we soon dropped this strategy and developed different ways of introducing measurement tools, reacting to coachees' requests or reported experience of them, or letting go of the whole area altogether.

Some coaches rely on an area of specialist knowledge they bring to the process. Assessment is just one example, but others could include knowledge of a particular industry sector, a sport, a job function such as marketing or a body of techniques such as neuro-linguistic programming (NLP).

However, coaching is a peculiarly 'empty' discipline: it borrows theory; its practice involves holding back; what coaches do *not* do seems as important to success as what they do. I regularly hear a comment like: 'So you get paid (a lot of money) for listening to someone then doing nothing: I think I'll become a coach.' Coaches can be particularly prone to imposter syndrome. People who suffer from this tend to devalue what they have achieved and not only feel that they are a fraud but that sooner or later everyone else will find them out. Success is down to luck or robust cover stories. The term was first used in 1978 (Clance and Imes 1978).

Psychometrics offers a false cure for this malaise: a body of technical, numbers-oriented, often seemingly arcane knowledge and skills which can be mastered and used as a defence against external criticism and, more importantly, against internal self-doubt. At times it has been used in exactly this way by other groups: HR staff facing scepticism from other managers; young occupational psychologists with precious little understanding or experience of the world of work beyond short placements and textbooks.

Psychological measurement can, at times, offer the wrong support mechanism as it distorts precisely what the coach should aspire to be good at: openness to the other person.

Strengthening the Barnum effect

I was born on 12 June. My birth sign is Gemini. Drawing on a number of astrological sources, I might describe myself in the following way.

> Geminis like being with interesting people and holding intellectual conversations. They are deep thinkers who are not content with surface explanations: they want to get to underlying issues and meanings. They sometimes ignore

simple practicalities and concentrate on issues like spirituality and philosophy. They talk and write well and, despite their interests, are funny and enjoy themselves. But they should not be taken for granted. They follow their own internal journey and if someone gets in the way they may ignore them. This is not cruelty but a concentration on what they see as important. They trust people but once that trust is broken it can never be mended. They have few negative qualities.

Yes, of course, that is definitely me. It just omits how modest I am.

Astrology is believed because of the Barnum or Forer effect. This is named after the 19th-century American entertainer P.T. Barnum, who founded the Barnum and Bailey Circus. He was supposed to have said, 'There's a sucker born every minute' though there's no actual evidence for this. The 2017 film *The Greatest Showman* gives an idealised view of his life.

Certain flawed psychometric tools are successful because of the effect named after him. This identifies that people think descriptions of their personality are accurate even when, in fact, they are vague ones which could describe a high percentage of the world's population. If a recognised expert such as a medical doctor makes negative assertions about you, you are more likely to accept them than if someone next door happens to describe you unflatteringly.

The term was first used in 1956, although research into the effect started in the 1940s. The Barnum effect has been consistently confirmed in research studies and is found throughout the world. There are a number of fascinating, detailed aspects of the effect but from our point of view, it is important to understand that too easy agreement stifles insight and conversation. This is the other side of the statement I made earlier: 'respectful disagreement generates breakthrough thinking'.

This may be less of a problem than it once was. When questionnaire reports were first introduced by publishers there was a strong emphasis on only making positive comments and on keeping descriptions general. Negative comments were often described as 'areas for development' or 'more work needed'. More recent reports aim at greater precision and individualisation: assessment has increasingly aimed not just to praise but to challenge – another reason why they have a place in coaching.

But the Barnum effect still bedevils some assessments and some ways they are used.

Overinterpretation and stereotyping

I was attending the American Psychological Association Conference one year and was discussing the Myers-Briggs Type Indicator (MBTI), with an American psychologist. I stated that I was an INFP (Introvert, Intuitive, Feeling, Perceptual); immediately a response came from behind me, 'No Ian, you're not an INFP; your strongest preference is INFP but that is not your identity'. By chance, a friend of mine who then owned the company which adapted and distributed the Myers-Briggs® assessment in many countries happened to be standing behind me and had overheard my misinformed dogmatism. His challenge signposted our tendency to overinterpret tests, to ascribe to them a certainty and comprehensiveness they could never possess.

It is absurd to claim that asking someone to answer some questions or rank some words – no matter how lengthy the process – could give a complete and accurate description of them and how they would act in every situation. Assessments elicit focused samples, not complete descriptions of behaviour and its drivers. But unpublished, commercial research I commissioned some years ago, suggested that many assessment users believed the particular tools, in which they first trained, measured areas that they were not designed to or able to measure. At its worst, they become a sort of cult; they are seen to explain almost everything about a person and their technical terms are used to befuddle the non-initiated and identify fellow believers. Assessments can encourage unwarranted certainty where doubt is both essential and a rich instrument for investigation. This is often not the fault of authors or publishers, and the same cult-like behaviour adheres to many aspects of theoretical and applied psychology.

Responsible training and instrument design attempt to overcome this bias. They will emphasise that results should only be used with other sources of relevant information in making decisions. This is particularly important in environments where high stakes decisions are being made: who gets a job; what teaching is planned for a child; how someone's mental issues are going to be treated. Trained coaches should be less inclined to translate a hypothesis into a certainty; to move in a single step from partial evidence to conclusion.

All measurements contain error. Measure your height six times and you will get a number of different results. Your true height lies somewhere in that cluster. A well-designed assessment will provide evidence of how much dependence you can put on the results of a test through a statistical description of the Standard Error of Measurement (SEM), which is explained in more detail in Chapter 7. This is a corrective to over-certainty. Assessments are no different from any form of measurement in containing error. However, well-researched and constructed assessments are preferable to other forms of decision-making and measurement because they are stringently developed and make this inaccuracy explicit through statistics. The user can 'put a hand round' the error and use it in their thinking. Unfortunately, this explicit acknowledgement is precisely the reason psychometric tools are often criticised as less accurate than other forms of judgement. To give one contrasting example, recruitment decisions based on unstructured interviews are as useful as tossing a coin, but this extreme inaccuracy is invisible to many.

Another danger here is that this certainty will result in stereotyping. I know several organisations where participants wear badges at planning meetings. These indicate their 'personality profile' as defined by the MBTI framework. These organisations claim that this allows them to share a language to discuss and understand disagreements, to create a healthier climate of understanding, to improve co-operation and therefore performance. While these aims are important, the use of badges (or, in some cases, tee shirts silk-screened with personality profiles) can encourage damaging stereotypes and stems from a misunderstanding of how this sort of data can be used helpfully and of what a particular tool is measuring.

Seeing numbers as the truth

We trust quantitative research results. A percentage seems to tell us more than the words 'very' or 'a lot' or 'exceedingly'. Yet we also know the saying: 'There are lies, damned lies and statistics'. Recently we have become more aware of how numbers can blunt questioning and give the impression of greater certainty and precision than actually exists. Rather than discuss this in too much detail, I will recommend *The Number Bias* by Sanne Blauw (Blauw 2020) which is an entertaining and illuminating read. I suspect many coaches will be sympathetic to adopting a healthy scepticism about evidence which is given credence purely because it is expressed in numbers.

Seeing assessment as an end in itself

In coaching, assessment is never an end in itself. The results are only as valuable as the conversation based on them.

Assessment in coaching: for or against?

It might seem that these latter are compelling reasons for avoiding assessments in coaching, but the first part of this chapter made a strong case for using them.

You could critique other techniques that coaches use in similar ways. Most forms of specialist expertise can lead to over interpretation, simplification and control. I once mentored a sales manager who was a self-proclaimed expert in NLP. At a certain point I had to halt our conversation and ask him to stop using mirroring techniques to manipulate me; and also to stop basing sweeping and mistaken conclusions on my body language. The latter is an example of this issue: most of us can see how, used carefully, a knowledge of body language can contribute to effective coaching; over-reliance on it reduces the complexity of human individuality to the twitch of an eyebrow. Over-reliance on assessment can reduce that complexity to a few adjectives or a few numbers.

2 Using assessments in coaching

It's often suggested that 'no-one asks to be assessed'. Commercial research I commissioned some years ago showed this to be a mistake. The results suggested that some people love doing personality assessments, in particular, and jump at the opportunity to find out more about and talk about themselves. But the statement that 'assessment in coaching must always be voluntary' is of paramount importance. If it is not, the balance of power within the relationship will be disrupted and it is unlikely that the coachee will respond with the right degree of commitment and accuracy.

'Psychological contracts' became common in organisations in the 1980s and 1990s. In addition to the formal contract of employment there was seen to be a 'psychological contract' between employer and employee made up of a range of informal, unwritten, principles and obligations. This is true of any type of relationship, including those involved in coaching. The imposition of assessment without assent seems to me to break the terms of any psychological contract in coaching.

When to use assessments

At the start

Using formal measurement tools right at the start of an engagement can limit their effectiveness but, by contrast, sitting down with an assessment report provides a tangible agenda and shared language which might help the 'getting-to-know-each-other' process and shorten concrete goal setting. Sometimes the issue the coachee and/or sponsor have raised and which the coaching process then addresses might lend itself to initial assessment.

> Sam was underperforming in a job. During an initial 'getting to know you' session, he admitted that he was thinking of applying for a new post even though he enjoyed his role and colleagues. He wasn't sure what he was missing.
> I suggested administering a motivation assessment. He had taken personality assessments and ability tests several times earlier in his career and was aware of some aspects of his personality profile. He had enjoyed the

experience and was interested in looking deeper: he felt this would contribute to his work but also to help him make choices about life outside work.

Discussing the report that the assessment generated led to an immediate breakthrough, Sam's boss was trying to motivate him with external rewards (increasingly important-sounding job titles, pay rises, 'perks'). Sam wasn't demotivated by this, but they weren't actually motivating him to do more effective work or to feel more settled. Sam was driven by internal motivators. These included doing a job well, feeling he'd contributed something to the lives of customers and his direct reports, rather than external factors such as status, power or wealth. His work offered him some of these internal satisfactions but not enough. And his achievements in these areas tended to be downplayed.

With his agreement, Sam and I held a three-way meeting with his boss who was a sponsor of the coaching process. Together we agreed some changes to his responsibilities. Sam and I worked on setting and recording achievements that held meaning for him, achievement of which would provide him with satisfaction and further motivation.

This all took a couple of sessions after which he stayed in his job and his performance and job satisfaction improved considerably. However, this outcome raised issues in Sam's family life as these choices affected their income and lifestyle and the goals Sam's partner was aiming for.

Our motivations are often not clear to us. A coachee might well raise these sorts of issues at the beginning of a coaching process and here assessments offer one option for kick-starting discussions.

At other times

When might you use assessment if not at the start? To some extent this is situational – it will differ from one coach and coachee to the next, from one coaching issue to the next. I use assessments in a range of situations. One is when the third-party view of an assessment report might help both me and the coachee tackle an issue.

I was asked to coach Lena by her HR director. While Lena delivered excellent top-line and bottom-line performance for her strategic business unit, there was dissatisfaction among her colleagues. The problems related to Lena's communication styles with different organisational levels: with direct reports she tended to micro-manage; with her own managers, operating at a group level, she was desperate to explain her position rather than listen, question and understand their goals. She reacted over-emotionally to criticism. This issue had been highlighted by the company's own 360-degree appraisal system, which I had access to, and initial conversations with her.

A combination of a strengths inventory, an emotional intelligence questionnaire, a five-factor personality measure and Lena's CV confirmed the situation in a way which allowed Lena to begin to understand what she was doing. She was more at home with, and skilled in, using and manipulating numerical information. This had two important implications. First, she couldn't understand why people were unhappy when she was delivering hard, tangible, financial performance. Second, Lena was happy to take the large battery of assessments since they in turn provided feedback based on numbers and hard information.

Her numerical bias made it easy for her to calculate areas which presented less risk and which she could delegate to her direct reports and stop micro-managing. Since she could concentrate on a smaller number of high-risk tasks, her workload was reduced. This alleviated some concerns we'd discussed about her work–life balance and how it was affecting her family. Recognising this numerical bias also allowed us to talk through her tendency to use numbers as a 'weapon' in conversations with her managers and peers. We jointly developed a way of turning her numerical arguments into simpler verbal ones which could, if necessary, be backed up by numbers. It also allowed us to identify techniques for dealing with her tendency to get overemotional when her evidence-based arguments were not accepted: using breathing techniques was one. Lena prepared her presentations and arguments for meetings carefully: she always had the facts at her fingertips; I typified our ideas as a way of preparing behaviourally and emotionally for meetings in the same professional way.

Colleagues, her family and friends began to notice a change in her behaviour. While the focus of our coaching was work-related, greater self-understanding, improved health, less stress and less emotional lability had huge benefits for life outside work.

This example highlights that you should not use assessments in isolation. Lena's CV – which showed considerable experience in high-level banking and investment – gave strong evidence of why she felt so at home advancing numerical arguments and what was at stake in de-emphasising them, issues she had never acknowledged before.

I often administer assessments if the coachee asks me to. This happens more often than one might think. The trick here is to ask the person what they want to achieve through the assessment.

The preferences of the coachee are critical. I was put forward, along with a couple of other coaches, to work with different members of a team of organisational country managers. The HR director making the decision asked me to work with one person rather than either of the other two leaders who had asked for coaching. The reason she gave was, 'Anna will react positively to you because you seem more academic than the other coach who is a better fit with other managers'. Lay aside whether I warranted that description (I don't), different people prefer different coaches and different coaching approaches. That's why an initial 'getting to know you' session is so important. Some coaches like the numerically based, objective, scientific feel of assessment. It gives them more reassurance that coaching is an evidence-based practice rather than, at its worst, high-priced natter. A sensitive coach will quickly pick up this preference and also its opposite – a suspicion of being viewed as a test subject.

Assessments can help to break a log jam. They introduce an alternative view with which the coachee might agree or disagree. If the coachee displays no self-knowledge, if there is no common ground in the vocabulary you are using, if the model you are using has stalled, assessment allows you to approach the process from a different angle. It is not the only type of tool that can do this: any standard coaching technique (and some individualised ones – I've used my interest in poetry to achieve this, for instance) can help here. But assessment gives more focused information for a shorter time commitment than most other techniques.

These are my triggers for assessment. There are others. The key is to have a number of assessments available which you can draw on when the situation seems to call for a particular approach.

What to ask

During your initial meeting with your coachee, include questions about their experience of assessment. Here are the ones I suggest, with comments on some of the answers.

'Have you been assessed before?'

When do assessment results go out-of-date so that you have to consider administering the same assessment again? There's no agreed length of time, and different human characteristics change more or less quickly at different ages. Thus the cognitive ability of 5- to 11-year-olds will change quickly whereas the default adult personality will change much more slowly, though you change how you act depending on the social situation you are in: asking for a bank loan as opposed to attending a rave, for instance.

Using the same assessment or assessing the same area too frequently creates two risks. First, the assessment taker can learn how to manipulate their responses to their advantage; although this is more of a problem in testing for recruitment or clinical diagnosis. Second, and more importantly for coaches, too frequent assessment can lead to inaccurate results because the coachee is bored or blasé about the whole business. This can affect the wider coaching relationship. My rule of thumb is that I'm happy to use assessment results from the last six months unless a major change or problem has occurred in that time. If that is the case, or the last assessment was more than six months ago, I suggest re-administration. The deciding factor is what the coachee wants or is happy with.

'Can I see the results of earlier assessments?'

In terms of legislation and regulation on data protection and personal privacy, assessment data are no different from any of the other sorts of information you gather and store. It can be argued that adherence to legislation is more important given the specific nature of assessment results: administration is now largely carried out online and therefore data is stored digitally; assessment use is increasingly international and there are constant calls to move data between, for instance, different branches of international companies; stored assessment data is often numerical which suggests easier transportability; and assessments cover a wide range of often sensitive personal factors.

However, the same legislation and ethical principles will or will not apply to all the sorts of information you gather as a coach. Your coach training should at the least introduce you to any issues here and, if it does not, it is worth asking if your coach trainer, supervisor or accreditation organisation has guidance on the issues. A quick survey found fewer publicly available guides and more online conversations between members of different organisations dealing with coaching and data protection.

If you are particularly interested in data protection and assessment, the best places to look are the websites of the larger testing companies or, if you have access to them, national psychological association sites. In the UK, the British Psychological Society's (BPS's) Psychological Testing Centre gives guidance on a lot of issues, including a practical document on data protection in occupational assessment. Its guidance can be adapted for other uses. See:

https://ptc.bps.org.uk/sites/ptc.bps.org.uk/files/guidance_documents/draft_data_protection_psych_testing_in_employment_setting.pdf

This is only a draft guide. Data ownership and protection are hot topics. Rules are different in different countries and what's at stake (law enforcement demands for access to coaching data, for instance) will vary internationally. Governmental concern about social media and other digital technology companies' use of personal data is liable to fuel further changes in legislation. In the UK, Brexit has called into question the applicability of a range of European legislation including the General Data Protection Regulation (GDPR). Now the UK has left the EU, you can get government guidance on any changes at: https://www.itgovernance.co.uk/new-rules-on-data-protection. A chapter by Anne Stokes on this subject in *The Trainee Coach Handbook* (Watts et al. 2020) gives advice on how to ensure confidentiality for online coaching; these ideas can easily be adapted to apply to assessment.

But the implication of all this is that statements on data protection and privacy are all drafts and it's likely the rules will change regularly to catch up with digital innovation. Legislation and coaching seem to draw on different skill sets and concerns and maybe this is less of an issue for an industry made up of a few large companies and lots of small and medium-sized enterprises and self-employed people. Nonetheless, it's worth trying to keep up to date on these issues and, in addition to understanding the law, following your own ethical concerns on the use of personal data.

'What do you remember about being assessed before?'

The answer might be as vague as, 'Oh yes, I completed one of those test things many years ago when I applied for my job. I think I was a "blue" or something'. Other people might be able to describe their results in great detail. I find the answers indicate not only a person's basic attitude towards assessment but also that individual's comfort with self-investigation and self-evaluation. These insights will suggest whether assessments are an option. If answers are negative, it is worth investigating in more detail how earlier assessments were administered, fed back and used.

Responding to questions and comments coachees might make

'It's a new fad'

Assessment thinking originated more than 2000 and maybe as much as 4000 years ago, in China. Psychometrics emerged as a more formalised science in the 1880s at the International Health Exhibition in London. Many of the assessments used extensively now were developed around 70 years ago. You can argue the opposite to the suggestion that it's an unproved fad: psychometrics can seem a rather hidebound, old-fashioned discipline which has a focus on looking backwards built into its methodology. However, Chapter 8 will show some of the innovations that are disrupting this model.

'Is it science? It's like astrology'

Psychometrics is a specific area of psychology, developing out of standard academic research practice. Psychology itself is slightly ambivalent about its status as a science: many psychologists working in clinical, counselling and similar areas see psychology as an art or a combination of art and science. But both psychology and coaching emphasise the need for evidence-based practice: building interventions on research evidence.

Astrology is believed, when it's believed, because of the Barnum effect (pages 11–12). Psychometrics works when an assessment has been well-researched and records its accuracy and the extent to which it might be inaccurate.

'What about handwriting?'

Certain cultures use handwriting as a valid and reliable way of measuring personality. Trying to tell someone's personality from their handwriting seems only minutely more accurate than saying that someone's age will tell you what their personality is. We know that all 16-year-olds are not identical and that one 70-year-old will differ from the next 70-year-old in innumerable ways. Flipping a coin seems more accurate than either age stereotyping or handwriting analysis.

'Assessment simplifies people into a small number of categories'

'There aren't just 16 types of people in the world' is a criticism often made of the Myers-Briggs assessment. In fact, that assessment does not suggest that there are just 16 categories into which you can fit nearly eight billion or so people. To say that, or something similar about other tests, is to misunderstand both what is being measured and what is therefore being reported. This is even less of a problem in coaching use of assessment where categorisation is less important than insight and the reactions of coachees to a report based on their own responses.

Preparing to administer and administering assessments

Administering assessments became easier as digital technology established itself as the go-to delivery medium and as that technology has allowed assessment to become more flexible, subtle and, at its best, insightful.

For coaches, the ability to assess wherever, and whenever, the assessment taker finds most convenient is an unalloyed advantage. There is little evidence that the types of assessments coaches use will encourage 'cheating' or manipulation by the people taking them. If an assessment taker does distort his or her responses, a scientific assessment will flag this fact. Evidence of distortion can serve as rich material for coaching discussions about why the coachee felt they had to do this, what underlay the distortion and their ultimate goal. A major way to ensure assessment takers answer online assessments reasonably accurately is to introduce a mutual contract on the front screen. For coaches, negotiating initial contracts is a standard procedure and we can include assessment responsibilities in them. These could include:

- **Responsibilities of the coach**
  I will use only high-quality assessments
  I will use them observing all ethical, professional, and legal requirements including those relating to data protection and privacy
  I will give you a copy of your report

- **Responsibilities of the coachee**
  I will answer the questions/ give responses as accurately as possible, to the best of my ability.

How do you make sure you use an online assessment in a professional way to get the most accurate results and meet your responsibilities? Specific training, manuals, welcome screens and other sources will give you some information, but there are other issues you should consider.

You need to establish explicit agreement with coachees about why an assessment is being used: what the goal is, when you need it taken by and, if this is important, under what conditions it should be taken. Just like a coaching session, you don't want an environment so distracting that the coachee cannot react to the assessment with full attention. Filling in a personality test while standing in a crowded rush-hour train is not recommended; neither is doing it while suffering from a hangover (I draw on personal experience here).

You should explain the overall process and make sure you understand it. Different test publishers use different methodologies for administering, scoring and interpreting online assessments. For instance, some ask you for the email addresses of the people you want assessed and they handle the whole process, ultimately sending you and the coachee reports. In this case, the coachee may receive their invitation to take the assessment from the supplier – whose address they might not recognise or which their pc might consign to Spam or Trash. In other cases, you will have access to an online control panel and will send out the initial email, chase up anyone who hasn't filled in the questionnaires and other actions to make the process run smoothly. Some log on details may be time-limited so it's important to keep an eye on when people are responding (or not) to an invitation.

Once the assessment has been completed, you may get a report sent to you automatically or you may be able to choose which report you receive since different reports can be generated by the same base responses.

There are guidelines on the BPS Psychological Testing Centre website (see page 28). These International Guidelines on Computer-Based and Internet Delivered Testing are available at:

https://ptc.bps.org.uk/sites/ptc.bps.org.uk/files/guidance_documents/international_guidelines_on_computer-based_and_internet_delivered_tests.pdf.

They raise some of the issues but are now old in technology terms. Most guidelines on the use of technology in most areas of human activity are out-of-date before they're circulated. Treating assessments as another coaching resource and treating their use in the same way as you would other techniques will avoid most problems.

People with disabilities

Assessment manuals and websites should give you guidance on how to adapt an assessment to use it fairly with individuals with mental or physical disabilities. Your supplier/company contact should also be able to brief you. These adaptations can range from using specially modified response devices instead of the standard QWERTY keyboard or mouse to allowing a longer time limit. The latter is more of an issue with timed tests – for instance someone with dyslexia taking a verbal reasoning test at school – rather than the untimed assessments used by coaches.

The BPS Psychological Testing Centre (referred to in Chapter 3), has some guidelines on dyslexia, visual impairment, hearing loss and deafness.

What should you do if assessments seem to reveal a serious problem?

> During the phone call to Alan, a coach friend of mine, a manager at a major insurance company asked this extremely worrying question: 'By the way, how do I identify a psychopath?' The manager looked after the sales team of the company. and had a successful recruitment method, based on behavioural maps, which seemed to find exactly the right employees.
>
> One of the applicants for a sales job, let's call him G, had a great track record and fitted the behavioural map well. He was recruited and, at first, seemed to fit in well. After a few months, however, parts of his activity reports began to look suspiciously similar to those of his colleagues. He had a photo of his very glamorous wife on his desk but when he came to a company party with his wife, she was clearly a completely different person. There were other events that started to raise doubts about him.
>
> There was obviously a problem but the sales manager was keenly aware that he needed to be careful in dealing with G. Throwing around terms like 'psychopath' is dangerous and there could be less accusatory ways of explaining these behaviours. It might be that addressing them could solve any problems G was experiencing. The manager asked Alan to find out more information on what was going on and address any development issues that might arise.
>
> During the early stages of this process, Alan administered a range of assessments to G, including a personality test and measures which looked at thinking speed and problem solving. Based on these results, Alan could begin to model what was going on. G took a long time – sometimes a very long time – to process new information, to make decisions and initiate action. On the other hand, he was incredibly competitive, something he'd imbibed from his early family and school life. The assessments showed that in the very goal- and numbers-driven role he was in, he was having to behave differently from his natural style; so differently in fact that you could almost say he had two characters. One was the person he was projecting to his manager and colleagues; the other was an underlying one.
>
> Looking more closely at G's CV (which the company should have done during the recruitment process) it seemed likely that his relatively short time in any job resulted from this behaviour.
>
> I know that G was 'let go' by the company but it's possible that the coaching process and this identification of the situation could have helped him in future roles.

As this shows, when dealing with the possibility of serious psychological or behavioural issues, both false positives and the occasional false negative can have huge implications for the person in front of you and for your coaching relationship. It can also lead to ethical dilemmas around what the sponsor is looking to achieve by coaching.

This case study shows that results from standard personality and other assessments can help to clarify these situations. As we will see, certain specialist assessments may help if the coach is beginning to have concerns about a client. Here's another example. Some years ago, a leadership coach I knew measured an experienced CEO's thinking style, using an unusual, pioneering assessment. The results suggested his thinking was chaotic, an extremely rare result from this assessment. It seemed particularly odd given his long track record as a successful senior director, although recent roles had resulted in much less success. The coach investigated some different possible explanations for this from recent traumatic experiences to involvement in an industry sector that the CEO could not grasp. None seemed to fit the bill. Finally, after many sessions, the CEO came to a meeting in a highly emotional state and revealed that the large collection of empty whisky bottles he'd hidden in a locked cupboard at work had been found and reported. He had been put on garden leave to investigate his alcoholism and the company had referred him to a specialist in addiction issues.

Assessment reports tempt coaches to become amateur psychologists. This tendency is further fuelled by society's seeming fascination with psychological states, in particular those that are too often seen as disabling ones. Some years ago, there was a huge interest in psychopaths and sociopaths: this is reflected in the question asked by the manager in the earlier case study. The two are not the same but have sometimes been treated as though they were identical. This interest was initially fuelled by films about serial killers, then research data suggested that a far greater percentage of the population were psychopaths and/or sociopaths and that leaders of large commercial organisations exhibited similar personalities to those diagnosed with these conditions. Bookshops were suddenly stacked with titles like, *The psychopath next door*, *Are you married to a sociopath?*, *The psychopath in the board room* and *Are you a sociopath?* and non-clinical assessments were produced claiming to identify sociopathy. Some training courses and books on coaching suggested how quickly you needed to run if there was a hint of either condition in your client.

Hidden among all this brouhaha there were some genuine insights, robust data and salutary warnings. There are insightful books on the topic. The book first published in 2006 and revised in 2019, *Snakes in Suits: Understanding and Surviving the Psychopaths in Your Office* by Paul Babiak and Robert D. Hare, is particularly useful in learning about this area. My point here is how easy it became to label people as suffering from serious conditions; how easy it was to start spotting psychopaths in your firm, your past, your school, the mirror.

It is unlikely that any general coach will ever come across an assessment that reliably diagnoses these or any other serious mental condition. The 'dark side' assessments discussed on pages 63–65 do not claim to do this. They look at derailment within leadership personality under pressure: the characteristic but understandable reactions of people with huge responsibility and stress.

This is an extremely sensitive area and there is genuine disagreement about how to cope with such situations in both a professional and a human way.

When you begin to suspect a serious problem in the psychological make up of a coachee there are a number of ways of reacting. If this is during the getting-to-know-you phase, before a contract is prepared, don't take on that client. Most trained coaches possess a list of specialist organisations and individuals for client referrals on such occasions. Uncertainty is unavoidable in these circumstances and you can talk the issue over with your supervisor. I believe I have human as well as professional responsibilities in a coaching relationship and therefore coach the person as far as I can, being careful to refer them the moment I feel out of my depth.

Assessment feedback

At one time, learning how to give feedback – including extensive practice with volunteer students – was a major part of the agenda in assessment training. It was understood that feedback was a particular skill, essential whatever the purpose of the assessment although, in certain uses such as recruitment, feedback was quietly forgotten as too costly. Test takers were not given copies of their reports; test administrators explained to them what their responses meant and then answered questions if time allowed.

Without repeating many of my claims about coaching, you can see that it invites a different model of using assessment. In coaching use, a report is part of a conversation; it's a record of how the coachee has answered some focused written questions about themselves. In the coaching context, discussing these results is not a necessary duty or add on; it is the core of the process. So, test takers should receive their reports and coaches and coachees discuss them. Coaches use those techniques that are core to their practice: hypothesis; challenging; genuine questioning; listening and reading; silence; recapping. Even evidence of social distortion in the results – changing responses to make the assessment outcome more favourable – is not there to catch the errant test taker out; it's evidence to help the coachees examine their own behaviour, motivations and goals.

In coaching, assessment reports are not feedback. They are a further element in a conversation among equals. As a coach, you are trained to use information as the basis for genuine conversation and need no additional specialist feedback techniques related.

If you do want a slightly more detailed look at issues in feeding back rather than discussing psychometrics, Dr Almuth McDowell's chapter in *Psychometrics in Coaching* (Passmore 2012) is an excellent introduction.

Research

Coaching users increasingly use research evidence. They want to know if a particular coaching exercise 'worked' in helping someone move towards a goal. Coaching itself is becoming an evidence-based practice as its overall effectiveness is questioned. And coaches themselves often have an interest in research they carry out on their own practice, used in white papers, marketing pieces and in academic journals to bolster their brand. Assessment results can provide raw material for effectiveness research: they allow you to look at the movement of scores on a particular instrument between the beginning and end of a coaching intervention.

But interest in coaching research has increased slowly. The reasons range from the limited resources available to the self-employed or micro-company to lack of research expertise, to a suspicion of seeing clients as subjects. Coaches still seem to prefer case studies as a means of examining and explaining what they do – and these are, in their way, a form of qualitative research.

The best brief introduction to research in coaching I know is Sarah Corrie's chapter in *The Trainee Coach Handbook* (Watts et al. 2020: Chapter 10). If you read this and take what you know about assessment you can begin to consider how important research is for you.

3 Accessing the right assessments

Around 20 years ago I left gainful employment with a major assessment publisher and became self-employed. I contacted 10 to 15 assessment publishers to find out what was available, what I could train in, and therefore use, in my new work. The results were similar to what you'd have experienced from most industries at the time. Some didn't, and still haven't, contacted me. Some required a lot of my personal and contact information before they would even speak to me. Others sent me marketing information of more or less relevance. By contrast, a representative of one company made an appointment to see me at home. She turned up on time, asked me questions, understood that I had previous experience in the area and gave me a range of material on CD-ROM, including technical manuals, sample reports, research documents and marketing materials. She rang up two weeks later to check if I had questions and whether I wanted to book a training course. Since then, I have both used their assessments and worked with them on new developments.

Assessment is a big territory. Fortunately, there is now more online material that there was 20 years ago, from course notes to the websites of publishers offering much more background than used to be the case. How do you go about finding out more; how do you choose the right assessment for your purposes out of the many available; and once you've chosen the right one, what do you have to do to access it?

The place to start, for this as for many other unknowns, is the internet. Put 'psychometric tests' or 'assessments' into a search engine and the first pages of listings tend to be dominated by free 'test yourself' assessments of unknown quality plus sites offering tips and practice tests to job seekers. You will find similar sites if you put in more focused searches such as 'assessments of motivation' or 'personality assessments'. However, you can ignore these types of results and quickly come to more informative hits. For instance, when I put in 'personality assessments', the first page of results included two articles suggesting 'top personality assessments'. I disagreed with these listings in part but some lesser-known assessments looked worth investigating.

The websites of publishers vary hugely. The Myers-Briggs Company offers sample reports, research highlights, links to consultants, development histories and details of training courses. It's more like exploring a world than learning a subject. Perhaps this sort of marketing richness is another reason why the Myers-Briggs assessment is so popular among coaches. Some other companies take a similar open approach offering, among other material, assessment-related videos. Others are much sparer, offering marketing top lines and inviting you to talk to someone at the company or register an interest. At the least, a website should offer: sample reports, a manual or some description of development processes and research; what an assessment is used for and how old it is.

There are other sources of arguably more objective information. Some coaching accrediting organisations will provide guidance and briefings on key topics via their website; if you are accredited by a particular organisation, it will be worth talking to them to see if they have experts or formal guidance in the assessment area. The three key international accrediting organisations are *The International Coach Federation*, *The Association for Coaching* and the *European Mentoring and Coaching Council*.

As I write this there are a number of discussion groups about coaching and assessment online. 'Assessments and Psychometrics in coaching practice' is one such LinkedIn group I belong to. As with all such groups, it's important to adopt a critical stance, screen out below-the-line marketing and get to substantive information and discussions. These sorts of groups appear and disappear quickly so you may need to do some online research.

Psychologist associations

National associations for psychologists are often rich sources of information on assessment. In the UK this is the British Psychological Society (BPS), in the USA the American Psychological Association (APA). It is easy to find other national psychological association websites to find out their involvement in assessment and local policies for their use. Here I'll use the BPS as an example, partly because I am familiar with its workings, but also because it was a pioneer in extending use of assessments beyond psychologists. Its innovations have influenced other national and international associations.

The BPS was a pioneer in widening assessment use, creating a competency structure for assessment training designed to increase non-psychologists' skills. It accredited external training suppliers to deliver training courses, then quality checked them. The qualifications these courses delivered became nationally recognised, particularly among HR staff. There are two other areas of the BPS which can be sources of information and advice to coaches.

The Psychological Testing Centre of the BPS (https://ptc.bps.org.uk/) gives more information on this training structure. Its wider remit is to inform assessment users in various fields, promote best practice and raise the standards of assessments and assessment-related training. The information included on the site includes over 150 reviews of assessments, some of which are accorded registered status when they meet a certain technical standard. At one time it was common for organisational clients to ask if the assessment you were using was reviewed on this site. That it was reviewed was often, and mistakenly, regarded as meaning that the BPS approved an assessment. Because of this, publishers and developers were prepared to spend reasonable sums to get a favourable review and there was some evidence that this process was gradually raising the technical level of some assessments. These reviews are a source of assessment information but they need some explanation.

If you complete a BPS-approved course and pay to be on the Register of Qualifications in Test Use run by the Centre, you get free access to these reviews and the *Assessment and Development Matters* quarterly journal. You also receive these benefits – among others – if you are a BPS member. But if you are not a member, or have not completed a BPS-approved course, you have to pay for the full reviews. These are based on the model of the European Federation of Psychologists' Associations (EFPA). My view is that they are rather technically biased. People rarely choose to buy a car based solely on the technical specification of the engine: they take account of many factors that are important to them. The same is true of assessments where you should take more than technical aspects into account. The BPS assessment reviews star-rate a huge range of technical qualities and descriptive sections are often equally technical. They have become somewhat out-of-date in the last few years as assessments have become more innovative.

A different approach is reviewing as you would a novel or non-fiction book: descriptive, analytical, individually written reviews. *The Mental Measurements Yearbook*, from the Buros Institute at the University of Nebraska takes this approach but is expensive and the majority of titles reviewed in it will not be of interest to coaches. It may be worth searching out in more academic libraries.

A number of other national systems for review are based on the model created by the EFPA. This is being reviewed by the EFPA Board of Assessment (http://assessment.efpa.eu/board-of-assessment-/) which may in time become a rich source of assessment information. Its members represent a huge spectrum of national systems as does the International Test Commission (ITC: www.intestcom.org). Both organisations are changing at the moment to reflect the field they work in.

The Division of Coaching Psychology (https://www.bps.org.uk/member-microsites/division-coaching-psychology) is the other area of the BPS which will, in time, be of more and more interest. The BPS recently voted to change the Special Group on Coaching Psychology to a full Division, allowing psychologists in the area to become Chartered. It's also intended that psychologically informed coaches will be able to join, though the details of this have yet to be worked out. Other national psychological associations may offer similar arrangements.

Other sources of information

Publishers themselves have formed non-commercial groups similar to trade associations or pressure groups, designed to improve assessment practice, communicate with prospective users and influence national and international policy. The European Test Publishers Group (ETPG) (www.etpg.org) draws its members from around Europe and provides links to assessment publishers throughout the continent. These have to meet certain requirements about the quality of their publications and how they are supplied. I should make clear here that I helped found the ETPG and am presently involved with running it.

The US-based Association of Test Publishers (ATP) (www.testpublishers.org) is larger and more inclusive. Over its history it has helped set up sibling organisations in India (I-ATP), Asia (A-ATP) and Europe (E-ATP). Between them, these organisations offer comprehensive entry points into the range of assessments available and all claim to have high ethical principles. They are also involved in many conversations with psychological and other organisations which will influence the future of assessment.

The *Psychometrics Centre* based in the Cambridge Judge Business School is a major force in assessment innovation as well as offering training courses, assessment development software, opportunities for collaboration and a range of innovative assessments.

Choosing assessments

So you have read this book, done some general research using the sources I've mentioned and know some of the types of assessments that are available. You need to choose and train in an assessment/assessments to prepare for a specific coaching contract or because you need tools which reflect the issues and coachees you deal with. Before you think about registering for training, what sort of practical questions should you ask?

What do you want a particular assessment to do and is it designed to achieve this?

There are no such instruments as absolutely 'good' tests or assessments. When you read a marketing blurb using phrases like 'the best assessment' or 'technically the best assessment...' move on quickly. As with every other product or service I know – from plumbers to vinyl record players to cars or laptops – assessments are never absolutely good: they are good for a particular purpose or purposes and for the purchaser's needs, tastes, preferences and bank balance.

I will show that the Myers-Briggs assessment is useful in developmental and coaching functions but the publishers stress that it should not be used for selection or recruitment. There are more subtle reasons than the basic theory and approach why an assessment might contribute to one task appropriately and not another: assessment reports can talk a language that is incomprehensible outside corporations; some assessment items are written in ways which exclude some groups but which will appeal to others; some instruments are too hard hitting to use in the early stages of a coaching relationship.

The most important question you ask when choosing an assessment is, 'What is my goal in using this?'. This question requires dissatisfaction with the answers you initially come up with. Choosing a personality assessment because 'I want to find out someone's personality' is an inadequate reason. Why do you want to find out someone's personality? What will it contribute to the coaching process? More to the point, does the coachee want this resultant increase in or confirmation of their self-understanding?

People assess to find out the basis for action, not for the pleasure of impressing the assessment taker, getting the report, sticking it in a drawer and forgetting it.

Does the assessment suit you and your coachees?

You should look at a sample report – many assessment publishers include a download on their website – and see if the way it is written and designed, the language it uses and other features fit the way you do coaching, and the wants and experiences of your coachees.

Some publishers are reluctant to share actual questionnaires and questions. However, they should be happy to show you practice items that are intended to help takers get used to an assessment format and therefore respond in a way that truly reflects their situation. These are often items that were originally in an early draft of an instrument but were dropped during its development. They will give you a reasonable idea of the approach of an assessment. But the best way to understand what your coachee is likely to experience is to do the assessment yourself. Some publishers will allow you to do this online and send you your report. Some will require you to get feedback from a trained member of their staff or from a recommended consultant. Either process will give you a sense for how it is going to feel like on the other side of the desk.

A rule of thumb is never to administer an instrument unless you have completed it yourself and you've had your results fed back. A small financial and temporal investment at the start can prevent costly mistaken choices and enable you to give your clients more understanding coaching. You should note issues such as: whether you can leave the assessment and pick it up later on; if and when you can go back and alter initial responses; what the providers' data protection and privacy policies are; if the assessment only works on certain hardware and software and so on. The latter issue was critical in the early days of online assessment but is less so now. However, you should check whether an assessment system has been optimised for use on smartphones. Some have but some haven't and, increasingly, many people use smartphones as their default digital device.

Do you need to train to use it?

This is such an important question – so the last section of this chapter looks at the types of training available and what their benefits and downsides are.

Is it technically adequate?

This question would come first in many books on assessment, aimed at a different readership.

The key sources of information on this include the following:

A **BPS review:** check whether one exists. As I've suggested, if it does, it will answer many of your questions.

A **print or online manual:** most assessments come with instructions on how to use them. In some cases, this information will be included in the preamble to the assessment itself. However, manuals can and should provide a lot more information on how and when the assessment was developed, who it was trialled on and what its technical performance looks like. In recent years, for whatever reason, publishers have been more reluctant to provide this sort of information, particularly for more innovative assessments. They may have concerns about intellectual property or 'cheating' in the case of selection tests. They may be influenced by the IT industry where protection of a unique algorithm is critical to business sustainability. But this development is a backward step. I don't suggest the model used in an early edition of the British Ability Scales which I marketed: it had four, very heavy manuals! But I would argue that if a publisher or developer resists providing any sort of technical information you should think hard before using their product.

In addition to, or instead of, manuals some publishers supply separate case studies and updates of research/data gathering. Chapter 7 covers more detailed technical issues you should investigate: here are a few more general ones.

When was it developed and updated?

It is important that assessments are, wherever necessary, updated frequently. Within the old print publishing model this was difficult: we had a rule of thumb that assessments had to be revised every ten years, driven as much by costs as anything else. Digital delivery and developments in assessment construction theory make updating easier, arguably cheaper, and more necessary. In essence, if an assessment has not been added to, reviewed, had research carried out or revised for five years, then be careful about considering it. This is not just an issue concerning data. The acceptability of certain words and verbal forms is changing quickly. Using older reports risks giving offence to certain groups.

How is it scored?

The way many digital products work, from car information systems to Alexa, seem a mystery even to supposed experts. This is equally true of assessments now that they are largely digitally delivered. You had to hand-score old paper and pencil assessments and thus understand how the assessment worked. In digital versions, someone responds to items and a report appears as if by magic. At the least, it ought to be possible to understand how the scores were arrived at and who wrote and designed the basic statements from which the final reports are put together by software rules: was it an expert in the assessment; someone who knows about its subject; a team; a consultant?

What is the make-up of its norm groups/trial data subjects?

Well-packaged assessments are explicit about the group with whom the responses of an individual test taker can be compared. This is known as the norm group and you need to know what sorts of people are included in it: including the mix of nationalities, genders and when they were gathered. The key issue for choosing an assessment is not norm size but validity which I explain in Chapter 7. But if an assessment has less than 100 people in its norm group it may not be worth looking at.

How is the assessment delivered?

Most assessments that coaches will come across and want to use are now delivered online. Given that these are not being used to make high stakes decisions, such as recruitment to a job, the likelihood of 'cheating' is non-existent. Online administration is convenient, cheaper, eats less into face-to-face time and allows periods of reflection. This method of delivery has proved invaluable as coaching has become increasingly 'Zoomed' and 'Teamed' during the lockdown. Online assessing and coaching will continue after the pandemic – the benefits are too great. My point about taking an assessment before using it with others is particularly relevant here.

How do I get hold of adaptations and translations?

Many coaches work internationally or with a range of linguistic, ethnic and religious groups, and many assessments have been adapted for use in different cultures. I use the word 'adapted' deliberately. Assessments should not be translated word-for-word in the same way that a novel or report would be; they should be adapted to ensure they are measuring the same constructs. The International Test Commission has produced a standard for this process (https://www.intestcom.org/files/guideline_test_adaptation.pdf).

Even if an adaptation of a preferred assessments for a country you work in is available, check that it's easy to get hold of. Contractual relationships and local professional supply restrictions might make this difficult. Your local supplier should be able to answer any questions.

Can it fulfil more than one assessment need?

This is particularly true of general personality assessments which may drive a variety of reports: on resilience, emotional intelligence, motivation or values, for instance. This will save you time and money and reduce the cognitive load of learning four or five instruments.

How much does it cost?

Assessment pricing varies both in level and in how charges are structured. Some companies offer annual licences, irrespective of how often you use an assessment. Many use a credit or token system. This means you buy a number of these, sometimes with volume discounts, then are charged a number of credits for different operations: administration of the assessment; producing a report; overlaying team members in a team report etc. Some charge when you buy an assessment; some charge only when the assessment is completed and a report produced. This variety is made possible by online delivery and draws, at times, on IT industry practice.

Take your time in discussing with the assessment publisher the different options for charging – you might be able to get discounts for volume usage, supplying data, contributing to research or advising on product development.

Training in assessment

Since assessments come in all shapes and sizes, so do the requirements you have to meet in order to buy and use them. In certain countries, psychometric assessments can only be interpreted by qualified psychologists, that status being defined by initial training. Some companies require you to have gone on a specific course; others will give you access with no questions asked. Over the past few years, assessment training has been delivered in more flexible ways: in-person; online; blended. The online route has become much more common during the pandemic, reflecting a more general move in training delivery for many professional groups.

Open access

Assessments offered with no training requirement range from magazine infotainment quizzes to the free assessments which appear high up on any search engine list. Some of them are what they appear to be: fun quizzes about as stringent as horoscopes. Others provide an explicitly stated or implicit opportunity to practise filling out an assessment. The results in both these cases are irrelevant.

Some open access assessments are more than this. I recently filled out a resilience questionnaire on the Robertson Cooper site. I knew the organisation; they have an excellent reputation and I discovered some things about myself by taking the assessment. In other cases, I might have tried to find out more background information. Free assessments are often offered to gather data in research projects or as part of a survey: the BBC have offered open access assessments authored and developed by reputable developers on their website in the past.

On the whole, however, freely available assessments are of poor quality and may be loss leaders for other services. They should be treated with caution. In this area, price does at times signpost quality.

Assessment-specific training

Most companies offer assessment-specific training to allow access to assessments they publish/distribute. There is usually an initial course which qualifies you to use an assessment at a basic level. This may be one to three days long with some pre-course work (reading and actually completing the assessment). It may also require post-course work or check-ups to see that the skills you learnt are still being applied. Such courses should cover both the background theory of the instrument and skills you need in feeding it back and analysing the results. The technical content of these courses has declined in recent years and, for the most part, you need no previous experience of assessment to go on one. Equally, because administration tends to be online, there's less emphasis on how you administer and score instruments in a standardised way than there was when this involved a print assessment. There are huge numbers of variations in these courses: one company I know divides its one-day basic training into a half-day background introduction course and a half-day skills-based course. Others offer several formats for beginning to use an assessment. In my experience, one day is not enough to equip someone to use an assessment expertly: two days is a more appropriate length.

Increasingly, companies have created follow ups, courses and workshops which offer advanced training in the use of a tool, building on the initial qualification courses mentioned previously. Training courses for the major assessments described in this book often take this approach. It is particularly effective if you are using a reasonably complex or subtle tool regularly: training skills have a short half-life but also tend to reduce in effectiveness when overused. Being a 'master or expert' practitioner in a tool will improve its value to your coaching and looks good on proposals. These developments have been driven by commercial as well as academic concerns. Shorter courses prefaced by less technical explanation strengthen loyalty.

Some companies bundle together a range of assessments into one course. For instance, I trained with Team Focus on a range of tools specifically for coaches; this was cost and time-efficient. It would be sensible for other suppliers to take up this approach and direct courses to particular uses and users rather than focusing on one particular assessment, thus providing practitioners with a toolbox they can use flexibly.

Once you have found an assessment that you think will help your conversations with a coachee, you should identify the basic qualifying training course and ensure you understand what outcomes it offers, when and how it is delivered, pre- and post-course requirements etc. In addition to this, there are some specific areas to ask about. If you work internationally, does the course allow you to access the assessment outside your home country? Different countries have different qualification requirements. Does the course allow you access to different language adaptations of the assessment in your home country or outside it? If your profession requires continuing professional development, does the company help you link your training to that process? Equally, can you link assessment-specific training to the qualifications offered by the BPS?

Qualifications in assessment

The BPS's Psychological Testing Centre (https://ptc.bps.org.uk/, see pages 28–29) offers approved training courses based on its assessment user competence framework. The courses initially became much sought-after, nationally recognised qualifications, particularly by HR staff. They have changed a bit over the years but the present structure has three basic types.

Assistant Test User: available in separate versions for Educational, Forensic and Occupational test use. This qualification allows someone to choose and score tests but not choose or interpret the results.

Test User: available in separate versions for Educational, Forensic and Occupational test use. There are two different Test User Qualifications for occupational users – Test User Ability (TUA) and Test User-Personality (TUP). The Test User Ability course gives you access to ability tests generically: they address the same issues in much the same way. This course is usually statistically loaded. A TUP Qualification gives access to a certain type of personality assessment so you can go on courses and get qualified in different types of personality assessment.

Specialist in Test Use; only available for Occupational test users, this recognises skills and competences across a wide variety of tests and assessments.

The BPS also offers the Euro Test User Certificate which may in time become a means of recognising test user competence across Europe. Contacting publishing companies via the ETPG or ATP, or through their psychological associations, will alert you to any differences in supply and usage requirements in different countries. You can find a lot more, including a Test Users' Handbook, on the BPS website (at https://ptc.bps.org.uk/). There is no doubt that the structure the BPS runs – a set of test user competences, reviews of tests and verified training courses offering qualifications – has improved the quality of certain tests. The end point of all this, an International Standard in testing (ISO-10667), does exist and was revised in 2020, but has not been as widely adopted as was hoped. Despite this success in improving assessment use, these qualifications are designed for heavy assessment users: those who either use assessment a lot in large-scale occupational recruitment, selection and development programmes, or those for whom assessment is a core resource (in educational special needs work and forensic risk assessment, for instance). You will tend not to find them essential unless they would be valued as a badge of quality by the sort of organisations that buy your services.

So, while the BPS qualifications might prove valuable for certain types of assessment user, it suits most coach's needs to get assessment-specific training to access the best tools for their work.

Using other qualified users to deal with assessments.

Understandably, some coaches think time taken choosing and getting trained in assessments could be spent better on core coaching tasks. They delegate the whole assessment element of their work to a qualified assessment specialist. I have sympathy with this emphasis on outcomes but there are points which argue for spending time becoming an assessment user. These include the fact that third-party involvement might complicate or disrupt the coaching relationship. Not least, a dedicated assessment expert with specialist knowledge (but less knowledge of coaching) might disrupt the power balance in the coaching relationship. The more you use an assessment, the more you will understand what it is saying and this will increase the subtlety of your interpretations. This will not happen if you're simply briefed by another person. Coaches should take responsibility for their own assessment except when someone has been assessed quite recently before, within or outside organisations, and the results are available with the permission of the coachee. These previous assessment results can prove an initial bank of information to discuss close to the beginning of a coaching relationship.

4 The range of assessments

Which core questionnaires and techniques should coaches know about? In specialist areas of coaching, dedicated tools will be essential: an example is the wide variety of sports-related questionnaires, for use with individuals and teams. But there is a basic toolkit of assessment techniques which most coaches should be able to access and which will be of use across coaching applications. Your toolkit will need refreshing as you gain new coaching experiences and as the whole area of psychological evaluation changes.

Estimates are difficult to verify but there may be upward of 50,000 psychometric tests and assessments for a huge range of purposes, available internationally. How do you get to a manageable range of tools from this vast number?

Before focusing on the types of assessment coaches will feel comfortable using, I'm going to start with a brief review of those techniques that most coaches *cannot* use. This might seem perverse, but you will come across them in your work and they provide a wider context which we can then narrow down to more coaching-friendly assessments.

Types of test most coaches cannot use

When investigating psychological assessment, you will find references to tests which sound fascinating but which, on further investigation, you find you cannot buy or use unless you have specialist, high-level academic training or a particular professional qualification. These requirements often relate to a particular branch of psychology such as clinical, educational and forensic, or another medically related profession, such as speech and language or occupational therapy. As an example, some years ago, I published a test of mild depression which I found myself filling in when I went for a consultation with my GP. Although I had published it, I was not, in fact, qualified to administer or interpret it.

It is understandable why these tests are restricted. They can be used to diagnose mental conditions ranging from mild depression to schizophrenia and sociopathy. In schools, they can help identify learning difficulties and suggest a child may have conditions such as autism or dyslexia. Some tests evaluate the risk that prisoners pose if they are released. The outcomes of such measures can be treatment regimes, committal to a hospital, delays in prison release and access to specialist education. Some coaches who have also trained in these areas will be able to access such tools but, as a rule, most coaches don't purchase or use them. One of the keys to understanding this situation is the difference between tests and assessments.

Tests and assessments

I mentioned this difference between tests at the beginning of this book (page xiv). Jenny Rogers puts her finger on the difficulty here: that so many different words are used to describe the sorts of tools we're considering. She mentions assessments, tests, surveys, indicators, instruments and questionnaires as some of these names. Many of the books you might refer to use this variety of words in different ways and are more or less strict in their discriminations.

Tests and assessments are close family members; they are both techniques designed to measure. But provided we do not get too obsessed with minute detail, understanding their differences can help us to place specific tools and begin to understand what might be and might not be relevant to your work.

Tests

Most coaches tend to use assessments rather than tests. These two sorts of tools measure different human characteristics and are therefore used for different reasons. The primary evidence for this difference is whether the answers to questions posed in a tool can be considered objectively as right or wrong. If so, we're usually looking at a test. Tests are used in educational settings to measure what pupils know, where they have greatest potential and to help decide what courses they should take. In commercial settings they are used to recruit and, in some cases, decide whether to promote people. Different types of tests are used to diagnose mental health conditions and to qualify for a particular professional status. The written driving test used in some countries is another example from a different domain.

The measurement behind these uses must be accurate. You wouldn't want to employ someone as a copywriter if they couldn't string two words together – neither would that person thrive after such a misjudged decision. Making a mistake about an individual child's educational choices can affect their later life profoundly. It goes without saying that if a reckless driver passes the driving test, road rage sooner or later breaks loose. So, tests must be technically sophisticated and able to demonstrate the limits of their accuracy. They use a body of techniques which defines how you write, trial, score, administer and interpret them and quantify how accurate the measurements are and what differences between scores mean.

Tests tend to measure human characteristics such as knowledge, ability, skills. They ask questions or set tasks for which there are right answers.

Ability tests are the most commonly used examples of this approach in the general field of applied psychology, outside specialised clinical diagnostic tests (see Figure 4.1).

Figure 4.1: Types of ability test item

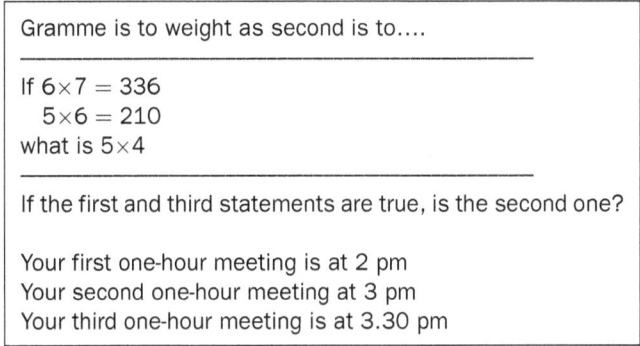

Figure 4.2: Structure of human abilities

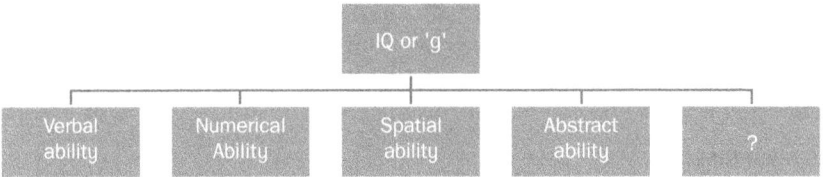

Measuring intelligence (often referred to as IQ or g) was, and still is, one reason for testing. IQ tests are used in some educational contexts, although rarely in commercial and non-commercial organisations. Their use has diminished for a variety of reasons, not least their earlier use in eugenics programmes and the mistaken contention that intelligence was a function of race or genetics. IQ is not genetic destiny nor is it related to the human quality of wisdom. IQ is made up of a number of different sub-abilities. These are shown in Figure 4.2. An ability is the possession of talents and skills that enable someone to undertake a particular kind of task successfully. We tend to test people for these different, more focused abilities in schools and in employment situations, rather than use IQ. Across populations, a high score on one of these sub-abilities tends to predict high scores on others. On an individual basis, however, we can have 'hilly profiles'. For instance, I score highly on verbal tests (you can decide whether those results are accurate by reading this book). On the other hand, my flat line spatial reasoning scores are reflected in the fact that my attempts to screw in a new light bulb result in several hours of Olympic gymnastic exercises and end with me lying on the floor surrounded by broken plastic, in continuing darkness.

These different abilities map onto specific jobs and areas of study. The question mark in Figure 4.2 indicates the possible presence of a wider range of 'intelligences' – identified in Howard Gardner's book *Multiple Intelligences* (2006). Their precise status is questionable. The other four ability areas specified are paradigms of what formal tests set out to measure.

In addition to objectively right and wrong answers, there are other 'symptoms' which suggest that an instrument is a test. They often compare individuals or groups with another group of people. So, a candidate for a role as a programmer might be assessed by tests of abstract ability and of their knowledge of a particular programming language. Their results will be compared with successful programmers already working in that role, as well as with other applicants. To make critical decisions about someone, or to fit them into a group, tests tend to emphasise numbers and their accuracy rather than words, which may offer subtlety but risk misinterpretation. Tests produce short reports built around scores rather than long ones containing commentary. Some are timed. Certain types of tests – the ability species I've mentioned above for instance – are designed to show the test takers best score, rather than trying to trip them up. They are tests of 'maximal performance' or capability, as opposed to assessments which show 'typical performance': the default way you act in everyday situations.

In other words, while tests affect the person being tested through the decisions made about them, results and reports produced by tests tend to be directed at the person who either sponsors or administers them so that they can make these difficult decisions accurately.

Assessments

By contrast, assessments were and often are seen as less 'formal' types of tests. This is not necessarily a fair description since assessments are often created using similarly stringent processes as are used with tests. This less formal typification stems from a number of issues.

People assess each other all the time in more or less informal events: a first date; the first meeting between coach and coachee; an informal interview for a job; a chance meeting on a train; looking at someone's handwriting or dress style. These loose assessments are open to all sorts of unconscious prejudice and distortions. Using more formal assessments, such as the ones I describe here, helps us avoid unconscious bias and prejudice, and ensures we know the limits of our judgements and therefore how much trust we can put in them. The key is to know which sort of assessment – loose or more formal – you're using and therefore how much you can depend on the outcomes. The claims made for some published instruments are heavily criticised because a desire to sell overcomes this need to be clear about what the instrument can and cannot do and what it should or should not be used for. Well-documented psychological tools give clear guidance on what their purpose is and how far you can trust what you deduce from the information they create.

It's now easy to create new instruments paying little attention to their accuracy but making them look attractive when they are delivered online.

Assessments measure aspects of human beings such as personality, motivation and values. These play out inside someone's head. Because of this, accuracy of measurement is less easy to achieve than when measuring specific knowledge areas which reflect our environment. Ability tests have objectively right and wrong answers: personality assessments, for instance, don't.

Therefore, assessment users accept lower levels of accuracy in their measurement and should be aware that they are doing this.

Assessments give those who take them the opportunity to externalise certain aspects of their internal life, look at their answers and – in the case of coaching – share them in the context of a trusting, focused discussion as a basis for discussion and action. Their results externalise the subjective. They are the third voice in a conversation. Answers to these sorts of questions express what strikes the person answering or responding as true.

Figure 4.3: Types of assessment item

Which adjective best describes you and which is least like you									
Happy	Inventive			Assertive			Sociable		
	Always			Often		Sometimes		Rarely	Never
I finish what I start									
	1	2	3	4	5	6	7	8	9	10	
Driven by detail									Driven by concepts

What is the 'symptomology' of 'assessments? Like tests, many assessments compare an individual's responses to those of other people, but they can also look at a person's individual priorities and preferences. For instance, some ask an individual to rank how important or how much they enjoy certain situations or aspects of their life or work, rather than comparing responses with those of other people (see Figure 4.3). Assessments can contribute to certain decisions; personality assessments often inform recruitment processes, particularly for more senior roles. But their emphasis in this context is more on generating interview questions to complement other sorts of information. More often, their results fuel development planning, training design and coaching conversations. Some assessments generate a number of different focused reports for different purposes: recruitment; self-development; coaching; and for different people – the test taker, the test user, the 'sponsor'. These reports include numbers, particularly in those intended for use by the test user rather than the test taker but emphasise careful interpretations of the numbers in words and diagrams.

Do coaches ever use tests?

As Jenny Rogers points out (Rogers 2019), ability tests can be useful in specific areas such as careers coaching. Occasionally, a test of ability might help a coachee in a business context.

Lois has a 30-year career in marketing. Initially she was successful. She was immensely creative in thinking up slogans and scenarios; her ideas for the place of marketing were original and resulted from a much-admired ability to ask simple questions which cut to the core of an issue. She collaborated closely with an unusually hands-on Financial Director in planning and evaluating campaigns. She moved from job to job, bolstered by her track record, but then consistently underperformed. Finally, one of her employers, a growing fast-moving consumer goods (fmcg) company, suggested she get some coaching.

Lois worried that she was 'too old in a young person's game'. She had not become bored with marketing but found increasingly that her ideas were turned down; she was not listened to and those campaigns that she created delivered diminishing returns. This had led to a deep unhappiness and one of her goals was to find an occupation which satisfied her. Financial rewards and seniority had never been great motivators for her.

The coach, with Lois's agreement, used a battery of assessments to see if they could identify the key issue. These confirmed some areas they had already discussed but one set of results were a revelation to Lois. The coach had suggested Lois answer a new battery of tests (rather than assessments), built around the range of abilities outlined in Figure 4.2. Lois's scores against the norm group of marketing directors showed, as the coach suspected, high verbal and critical reasoning skills. But numerical and abstract reasoning skills were extremely low. Lois at first resisted these findings but, over a couple of sessions, realised they showed exactly where the problem lay. The job of marketing director had changed during her career so that now it involved online and other digital methods and was judged far more by quantitative (and campaign post-mortems) rather than qualitative brilliance. Her immediate bosses, many of whom were younger than her, had grown up in this environment and Lois's commitment to words, concrete solutions and quality concerns impressed them not one bit.

Lois was simply in a job that had changed and no longer fitted her skill set. She and her coach set out on a process of discussing what options she faced to overcome this: get a new job; attempt to become more numerically and digitally literate; find a sector that valued her skills. These options became the basis for discussions of options and goals, and Lois's actual commitment to a forward path.

So, right/wrong tests can contribute to corporate and other coaching applications, but care needs to be taken in using them in this context. Many adults resent being asked to 'take a test which reminds them of school exams'. Some, particularly those with considerable experience and a sense of seniority, are offended at being asked to prove how smart they are when, in their view, they have nothing to prove.

Tests and assessments: a conclusion

There is a spectrum of types of tools which evaluate internal psychological traits for different purposes, ranging from categorisation and external decision-making to conversational support, treatment, description and market research. They are called a variety of names, not all of them neutral or even polite. But this distinction between tests and assessments shows that while some definitely do not fit with coaching's basic preconceptions, some do: in fact, their purpose is exactly the same as coaching. These tend to be called assessments.

In her fascinating book *The Hidden History of Coaching*, Leni Wildflower encompasses this distinction well and places it in a wider context. 'For centuries people have been weighed and assessed, most commonly according to social class or moral virtue. Non-judgemental systems for categorizing people are equally familiar...Twentieth century psychology gave a boost to both kinds of categorization – the evaluative and the value-free...' (Wildflower, 2013: 133).

I find that distinction between evaluation and value-free distinction an insightful way of thinking about the range of techniques available: tests evaluate, assessments are value-free. Wildflower goes on to confirm what I've observed: psychological measurement in many areas is moving from evaluation to value-free distinction; testing, including IQ and clinical diagnostic testing, is still used widely but more recent developments involve the creation of a huge number of genuinely rich non-evaluative assessments.

A definition

Based on the discussion in this brief chapter, here is my definition of the sort of measurement tools which will be of most use in coaching:

> A psychological evaluation appropriately used in coaching will tend to be value-free: it will make no judgements. It will externalise what is internal to a person and describe it in a way, a structure and a language that is inclusive and contributes a further voice to discussion and thought. It may be formal or informal; based on theory, empirical research or specific expertise and experience. It must be used with a purpose which reflects its characteristics and with an understanding of what it is measuring and how much its scores and description can be depended on.

5 Assessing Personality

Personality assessments are the psychometric tools most widely used by coaches. They come in all sorts of lengths and formats and draw on different models of personality: some based on theory, some on research, some on experience. These differences will affect how you go about assessing the area and then addressing what you discover. Investigating this range, training in and choosing different personality assessments for different purposes can be a time-consuming, complex and expensive business. This is one, but just one, of the reasons why many coaches, particularly those setting up their practice, will train in and use just one personality assessment. This is usually based on type theory and is most often the Myers-Briggs Type Indicator (MBTI). This type of approach is invaluable but should be supplemented by a tool or tools from a different tradition.

The number and diversity of personality tools reflects how the concept developed and the fact that there is no generally accepted definition of personality and how it operates. This might seem like a problem but you can also see it as offering coaches genuine choices to match different approaches.

What is personality?

Personality is not an organism bred in the laboratory or study, then released to dominate an academic ecological niche. Non-academics have talked about personality and labelled each other throughout recorded history. One of the best ways I've seen personality defined is the idea that it is 'the style of doing things' (Smith and Smith 2005).

A recent paper (Mobbs 2020) reported 20,699 English words descriptive of behaviour, building on earlier large catalogues. One major intellectual route into personality assessment has been to select from the thousands of terms used in everyday life and the arts, a much smaller number of which are precise enough to describe genuinely discrete building blocks of individual behaviours. At times, researchers have tried to invent words, spawning grotesque verbal creations: alexithymia (the inability to express emotion) is a favourite of mine. At other times they have taken everyday words and tried to redefine them slightly to be more precise, leading to a lot of misunderstanding and the need for great care.

Personality is a relatively stable guide to how we think and feel which, in turn, influences our behaviour. We recognise such a pattern in ourselves and in others. Such patterns do change over time and in different situations. In fact, it can be argued that each of us has several such patterns, but they are structured. Personality is not a self-regarding fiction designed to clothe our self's incoherence. This latter has been the view of some psychologists as well as experts from other disciplines and some post-modern creative artists. To amplify this: most people know that their default emotions, thoughts and behaviours – their 'style of doing things' – change for different situations. When they talk to their boss or a bank manager, they present a different pattern to the one they present to a close friend, a lover or a work colleague. Personalities also develop as individuals get older. Yet through all these short and long-term adaptations there is a consistency. I recognise certain characteristics in how I think, feel and behave from situation to situation and from year to year: they change in some respects – but I can predict some ways in which I will react, whatever the circumstances. People can do the same about others: describe some characteristics that express themselves in most different situations and use them as the basis for prediction. One of the first actions people take when they meet someone is to apply personality language to them. It is well known that these initial judgements are often influenced by completely irrelevant and sometimes damaging factors and prejudices such as appearance, weight, hair colour, age, ethnicity and gender. One motive for using psychometrics in certain high-stake decisions, such as recruitment, is to negate these subjective biases, to comply with equality laws and get a read of personality which includes an estimate of how right or wrong it might be. Off-the-cuff, informal, initial judgements and the words that enshrine them may change as someone gets to know a person over time, but most of us have an instinct that a person can be defined through a personality description which we will recognise most times we meet them.

Personality is like a late 19th century classical symphony or certain sorts of jazz: it has a theme which goes through a set of highly structured variations, yet sometimes goes off in unexpected directions. Another useful image is that while personality does express itself differently in different situations, overall it moves and changes, more like a pre-global warming glacier than a river.

Personality is sensed: its internal workings are induced from behaviour; too much theorising can work against common experience.

To sum up, what are known as the implicit theories of personality – the ones people develop about themselves and others – can be as important in some areas as more formal personality theory, developed in universities and clinics. In coaching, these views, which coachees themselves express, are primary material for conversation, and the imposition of an external theory can harm their self-insights and the trust that is central to the coaching relationship. The implicit theories that coachees hold about their own personality are central to the process as they are not in, say, recruitment where an objective view is privileged.

This understanding is important in explaining why certain assessments suit coaching. That an instrument like the MBTI assessment is criticised technically has to stack up against the fact that it is more sympathetic to how people think about themselves than some other measurement approaches.

All of these points in turn affect how we need to treat personality descriptions, whether given as informal off-the-cuff statements in a bar or meeting room or as the result of a more formal personality assessment. Such descriptions give us insights but not the whole story. They surface fundamental drivers of how a person acts in the world: the theme on which different situations and conditions play sometimes complex variations.

All of this provides a context as to why certain types of personality assessment appeal to coaches more than others.

Figure 5.1: Some types of personality assessment

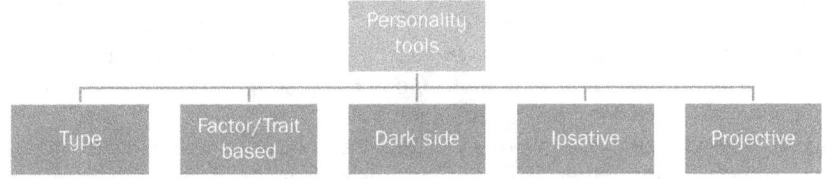

Figure 5.1 shows a standard way of describing the different types of personality assessment.

Type measures

'He/she is that type of person' or, 'He/she is typical of someone in that job/with that background'.

We use the words 'type' and 'typical' all the time about people, what they do and how they do it. Sometimes this has a negative connotation, as in the frustrated exclamation, 'Typical!'; sometimes it is neutral, as in, 'This is a typical example of a successful adaptation to the environment'.

'Type' is used as a shorthand to distinguish one group of objects from another or one category of person from another. Bases for this typing can be various, eccentric and non-exclusive: we use different ones at different times. Type models have influenced societies and disciplines widely. Hippocrates' application of the earlier idea of 'humours' to human health and temperament in the 5th century BC, was developed further by Galen in the 2nd and 3rd century AD. The fundamental idea was that four liquids – black and yellow bile, phlegm and blood – combined within the human body. If they were in the correct proportion and strength, the body was healthy; if not, the person was unhealthy. The continued use of words like phlegmatic and bilious evidence how long-lasting and influential this theory has been, and how it gave rise to four different types of human attitudes to life or temperaments. In the late 18th century, Johan Lavater initiated the pseudo-analysis of skull shape, which developed into an analysis of bumps on the scalp, to identify personality types.

Over the centuries, people have developed many systems for linking body types to personality, mental illnesses and criminality.

That these examples have been disproved as damaging pseudo-sciences should not cast a shadow on all applications of type to describing people. The use of the word *type* in psychology is simply an application of something human beings do universally: look at other people and, on the basis of certain criteria, seek to describe them and identify commonalities and differences. This habit can be misused, as in racist and sexist abuse, or serve as an accurate guide to a situation if the type system used is appropriately developed and proven. Effective type instruments apply this human urge to build instances into predictive and descriptive models in the latter, stringent, careful way.

If this were a book for occupational psychologists or HR managers, particularly those who spend a lot of their time using tests in recruitment, type measures would probably not be given first place in any discussion of personality measures. Type measures are never, and never should be, used in recruitment because of their technical qualities.

By contrast, coach training courses often highlight the MBTI assessment. I have yet to meet a coach who does not know of it or claim to have used it. That the majority of people I have met in business claim to have taken it is the flip side of this popularity. Over-familiarity can lead to boredom. This popularity seems to prevent coaches investigating other types of personality assessment.

In *Coaching with Personality Type*, Jenny Rogers (2017) looks at the use of types for coaching in detail. It is the best book I know on the relationship between the two areas and gives rich case studies, so I will not try to compete with it. My description of the type approach is therefore briefer than it might be. It uses the MBTI assessment as the core instrument, but I have referred to the features of other type measures where appropriate.

Background

In his book *Psychological Types*, published in English in 1923, Carl Jung suggested that three pairs of dichotomies comprised the elements that make up our personalities (Jung 2016). This insight came from a theory developed during his practice as a psychiatrist. Katharine Briggs read Jung's book which in turn influenced her work on temperament. Her daughter, Isabel Briggs Myers, contributed to and took over the research effort which resulted in the Myers-Briggs Type Indicator (first published under that name in 1956).

The tool has been revised, extended, adapted and researched hugely since then. The present European edition is formed of forced choice questions asking you to choose which of four descriptions best describes you. This results in a profile against four pairs of opposite preferences; Briggs and Myers added a fourth to the three that Jung had originally proposed. Rogers' book mentioned above, and material produced by the publisher, goes into a lot of detail about these; I'll give shorter descriptions.

Extraversion (E) vs Introversion (I): Your preference here (as in many assessments that measure Extraversion/Introversion) does not denote whether you are shy or the 'life and soul of the party'. Rather, it suggests whether you get energetic surrounded by people and contact or, by contrast, need to recharge your batteries in private after any exposure to others. This preference will underlie a number of behaviours such as how you prefer to communicate. I've long used behaviour at meetings as an initial sighter on this preference. My former boss once worked for a controversial publishing tycoon who would hold 18-hour meetings and end up bouncing around with energy while others were dozing with their heads on the desk. His preference was E. If your preference is I – like mine – you need to get away from meetings every 50–60 minutes to be on your own. In the past, I'm afraid I used my smoking habit as an excuse to take a break! But I hasten to add that I gave up cigarettes some years ago.

Sensing (S) vs Intuition (N): What do you first notice around you – things which you sense or ideas you 'jump to'? Do you get excited by the taste of a new sauce? In thinking about COVID-19 do you pore over data tables and – as some people I know have done – keep a daily record of numbers? By contrast do you get excited by an idea, a meaning, a way of doing things? Do you initially develop theories because they feel right and, surrounded by people whose preference might be S, have to find concrete evidence to back up your intuition?

Thinking (T) vs Feeling (F): This is about decision-making; whether you are objective and logical or, by contrast, whether you factor in the personal – relationships, other people's needs. These two ways of making decisions particularly impinge on different styles of organisational leadership.

Judging (J) vs Perceiving (P): How do you go about your life? Do you organise, plan, set goals, make decisions or are you swayed by events and what happens? Conflict in this preference can be a major point of friction in businesses, sports teams and in formal and informal personal relationships. One couple I know illustrates this J/P dimension. One partner prefers to plan a holiday down to the last detail, six months ahead; packs a week in advance; has the documentation in a set of carefully labelled plastic files and sets off in the taxi to arrive at the airport an hour before check-in opens. The other says 'Whatever', wakes up late on the day of departure, chucks stuff in a plastic bag and arrives at the airport to meet the other partner as the last call for their flight is made.

Depending on how you answer the items you will find you have chosen one from each of these pairs of preferences. Your personality type is denoted by the four letters of the preferences you have chosen. There are 16 possible combinations of these letters. Every time I have answered the instrument, my initial preference has been INFP (Introvert, Intuitive, Feeling, Perceptual).

What is it actually measuring – a question that should be asked of any test or assessment? In the case of the Myers-Briggs assessment, if your code is ESTJ or any other combination, what is the test describing and therefore how can it inform the conversation the coach and coachee get involved in? I've tried to stress the most important point: this sort of psychological typing does not describe what someone 'is'; it proposes what someone says they 'prefer'. In other words, every human being will both judge and perceive; will occasionally need company to be energised and will sometimes need to recharge on their own. It's just that each one of us prefers one side of each opposition and is in more control of it; but we can and will use both ends every day. Our preference is a default mode; from a coaching viewpoint, developing and strengthening the non-preferred sides of the dichotomies takes more effort. In its basic form, a good type assessment will tell you what that main preference and others you default to might be, but not how strong they are.

Questions to ask about any personality measure for coaching

Jenny Rogers' 2017 book, mentioned earlier, provides a measured account of why type measurement is so popular in non-judgemental assessment, while still being subject to academic criticism. You do not have to search far to find the latter. Equally, over-the-top praise for such tools is never far away.

If coaches want to use any personality tool, they should have answered a number of core questions. How does a type measure, using the MBTI tool as the example, stand up to this questioning?

Is it people-driven?

Is it driven by the person filling it in, an external theory or pure research? Will it support a coach's relationship-driven practice rather than, as a different approach might, cut across it or create distance?

Type tools are often described as being theory-based. In particular, Jung's original book can be typified as offering a theory of key elements in human personality with no formal research evidence. While this may be true in some senses, Jung's theories were based on his own clinical practice: the psychoanalytical sessions he held with many people. For me, this background qualifies as a sort of in-depth qualitative research, though it took place outside the confines of present scientific models. It developed from case studies: it is an eyeball-to-eyeball not an eyeball-to-microscope approach.

But there is more to being person-driven than just how an assessment was developed. For instance, does it talk a language that coachees can actually understand, which derives from their terms of reference, or does it try to blind them with science? This has been a problem with earlier assessments because of the way sessions were managed, how instruments were developed and by whom, and the sorts of words the reports used. The MBTI assessment and other type reports are often easier for test takers to read and understand, partly because of their language, partly because of the way type works. Because of this, the approach has sometimes been criticised for saying nothing. This is a question of taste rather than objective scientific finding. Reports for different types of instruments, written in the 1980s, were anodyne. This stemmed partly from the reverence of certain psychologists for numbers, allied to a fear of the capacity of subtle language to create imprecision. I published some reports like this myself. But the person responding to an assessment should be able to understand the report it generates, even if that understanding often needs some initial guidance from a trained interpreter such as a coach. Many type reports meet that criterion.

The area where the Myers-Briggs tool embodies coaching's people-centredness best is in how it is often used, an approach developed over a number of years. As I mentioned earlier, testing and assessment developed as something done **to** people, and assessment takers' views on their own personalities, were viewed with suspicion and 'corrected' using statistical methods. This situation has changed and assessment users can rectify the condescension of much past assessment by sharing reports with test takers. Some assessments provide different versions of their reported results for the assessment taker, the assessment administrator and others. The Myers-Briggs assessment process privileges assessment takers' views about their types, asking them to predict what their results would be and then welcoming a best-fit process to see how that estimate and the assessment results relate to each other. It does not dumb down results for the client. It assumes that someone's implicit theory of their own personality is a valuable piece of information. This process embodies a more realistic view of the role of assessment in coaching than some others.

Is it technically adequate?

This is another key issue – or rather two related ones.

The first is whether any particular assessment is technically adequate. Can it actually do what it says it can? Is it a vacuum cleaner that blows when it says it sucks? Any of the assessments I mention in this book can be examined in this way.

But there is a wider issue which concerns the whole idea of type rather than its specific application in one product. Most things, including psychological characteristics, create a bell curve – a normal curve of distribution – if plotted against the number of times it occurs. In other words, you find more examples or people clustering round the centre than you find at the extremes. As an example, if you plot the height of the general population in the UK, you'll find many more people who are around 5 feet 10 or 6 feet than you will at 3 feet or 8 feet, where the number of examples is small. The shape of this plotting is known as the normal curve of distribution (see Figure 5.2).

Figure 5.2: The normal curve of distribution

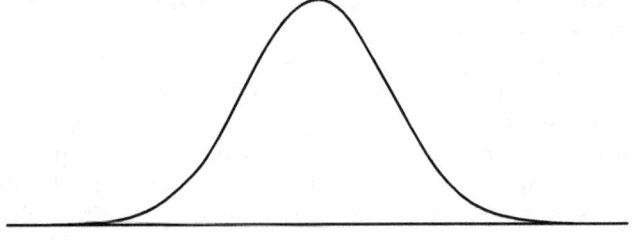

If you measure psychological constructs, you will see this pattern.

By contrast, type measures assume that the majority of people appear at either end of a scale: there is a definite mid-scale dividing line between two preferences. If you plot the incidence of a type characteristic you should get a shape like this.

Figure 5.3: Bimodal distribution

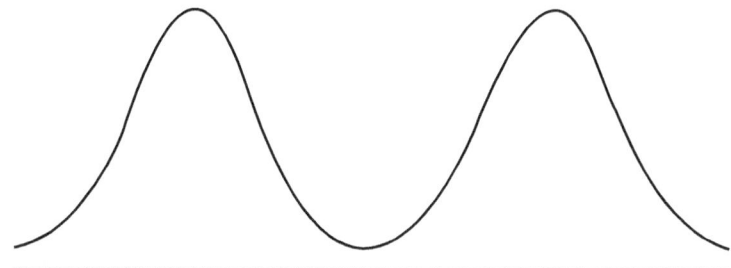

This seems odd. A lot of research fails to show a bimodal distribution, such as that in Figure 5.3, for the areas that type instruments measure: they show the standard normal curve of distribution. Given this, do we actually know what we are measuring? Can we judge how accurately we are measuring it? Aren't we just using the hunch (admittedly of a clever set of people) and dressing it up in numbers?

I suspect not. As Jenny Rogers (2017) points out, the experiences of many coaches suggest that MBTI, for instance, does give consistent results over time and between users. This technical anomaly is important but it is balanced by evidence from many coaching uses.

Who created type theory?

There is a large amount of criticism of the MBTI assessment stemming from the fact that it was created by two non-psychologists with no academic training in psychometrics. There was a strong sexist element in some of these criticisms which should thus be discounted and always challenged.

Perhaps less noticed is the fact that Jung, the originator of the theory, is hardly an icon for those psychologists and psychometricians who view their discipline as a hard science, only to be undertaken by those with the appropriate qualifications. Sceptics see a lot of Jung's work as a type of philosophy or theology (bad) rather than science (good). Jung, like other pioneers of psychoanalysis, has undergone considerable debunking in the last decades and, more recently, originators of testing theories such as William Moulton Marston, one of whose 'crimes' was his creation of the cartoon character *Wonder Woman*, have been the subject of best-selling biographies. It matters who has developed an instrument and how. In the 1970s and 1980s, a number of cultish organisations developed quasi-personality assessments, for instance. But the way to work out whether an assessment works is not via ad hominem attacks – the sort that have been consistently mounted against Katharine Briggs, Isabel Briggs Myers and others. Coaching is a rich and innovative discipline because it draws practitioners from hugely diverse areas. Psychometric pundits should welcome a similar diversity in their assessment developers and authors where they can find it.

Is it too simple?

You often hear the statement, 'The MBTI assessment says you can divide the world's population into 16 kinds of people'. This is wrong. Even at a basic level of description, a type indicator indicates preferences which can vary situationally. Myers-Briggs Step II® which divides each of the dichotomies into five further facets adds further subtlety to type descriptions, as do the concepts of type development and type dynamics – the extent to which we change as we grow older and the extent to which the dichotomies interact with each other.

The MBTI assessment is too often interpreted at a basic level. This is a problem with much test and assessment training: first, what you learn seems to have a short half-life unless it's reinforced by frequent usage; second, many people seem to be happy with using the basic version of what they've trained in and are continually pressured to simplify what they say about it. This is not just an issue for assessments though. Coaches should, through high-quality training, learn to value the importance of subtle meaning, the complexity of words, the power of waiting: and they should apply these lessons to assessment as much as any other area of their toolkit.

Does type help change?

When I was starting to work in testing and assessment, I walked into the office of the HR manager in a major public sector organisation. I stopped to look at the main poster on the notice board above her desk. It featured a grid of 16 characters from the then most popular soap on British television – *Coronation Street* – linked to a series of labels. What the HR manager had done was to ask the employees of the organisation to link the 16 MBTI assessment types to characters from Coronation Street, making the types vivid, relevant and memorable. I seem to remember that I shared preferences with a character called Ernie Bishop, but memory might be playing tricks. At the time, having been newly indoctrinated with certain ideas about how assessments should be used, I saw this as simplistic and rather silly (despite the fact that I was a devotee of that particular programme). In retrospect it was clever and the publishers of the MBTI assessment in particular have more recently provided a huge range of support material which relates the type preferences of different individuals to their interests in areas such as gardening, cooking and beyond. This can trivialise but there is also a fundamental reason why this approach can help coaches.

Coaching is about change: if change is not already happening or needed, it is unlikely a coach would be necessary. And one of the aims of coaching is to create change which is sustainable, which fuels the creation of new habits over periods of time. This process depends on memory and energy.

Ask anyone who has taken a type measure and they will probably recall their four-letter type as I can. While I can recall the overall drift of the results, I cannot remember the specifics of my profile on any of the other species of personality assessment I deal with in this chapter. Being memorable is a hugely powerful attribute of assessment outcomes, as it is of a song, a work of art or, indeed, a person. It is unlikely that change will be instigated or sustained by a third-person report in passive-voiced, abstract, scientific language treating hundreds of characteristics. Many type measures provide descriptions that are memorable, coupled with a range of ways of understanding, studying and relating them to you as an individual which are genuinely motivating.

There is a downside to this. Some tools overdo their packaging, hiding technical weakness and a seeming refusal to give any indication of how they work under whizzy graphics and simplistic, vivid messaging. The obverse side of engagement is labelling, trivialising and cultishness. Type measures are not unusual in this respect; major tests and assessments can create an unquestioning cultishness and evangelism, as can certain psychological-based movements such as neuro-linguistic processing (NLP).

But many type measures create memorability, simplicity and vividness. They provide explanations of how they work, warnings against misuse allied to material that energises and individualises with, in the best cases, no oversimplification. They support the process of change that is central to coaching.

Other versions of type

The popularity of MBTI often masks the fact that there are other type measures. Some seem to be little more than direct clones: others, however, offer slightly different functionality, ways of measuring, supporting resources and underlying assumptions. Some were created to correct the mistakes and problems many critics have identified in MBTI. In her book *Coaching with Personality Type* (Rogers 2017: 40–47), Jenny Rogers discusses eight of these alternatives which are of varying usefulness and technical quality. You can find others on the web.

There are some areas to look out for. Some of the alternatives add other perspectives to the basic Jungian one extended by Briggs and Myers such as the Keirsey Temperament Sorter®. Other alternatives, such as the Jung Type Indicator, tend to rely more on Jung's original thinking and attempt to overcome the bimodal issue. The Type Mapping System was created by someone with huge knowledge of Jung's work, seeking to introduce some of the subtlety and complexity he sees in the original theory into a tool which challenges some of the preconceptions that psychology brings. Lumina Spark is relatively new and comes from an applied background. Perhaps this explains how innovative it is in approach (combining type with some other models) and design. It also makes more creative use of technology than older tests, an issue which is of huge importance to the future of testing, particularly helping to ease the often-complex process of team analysis.

You will find other type measures online. More will be created over the coming years. Since the MBTI approach is so successful, many publishers of tests for business use seek to emulate that success with a competing instrument.

Summary of type

The technical issues with the type approach call into question the status of what is being measured, how accurate those measurements are and the relevance of type theory to the already debated concept of personality. The lack of evidence to support bimodal distribution is striking but so is the lack of support for type dynamics and type development. These are not trivial issues for a measurement tool.

However, technical concerns are not just the preserve of type measures. Any instrument, based on any theory, is open to genuine questions about certain of its measurements. Assessing personality never offers the same degree of certainty as testing temperature which itself, like all measurements, contains error. The key issue is whether the tool makes visible its workings so that prospective users can decide for themselves whether the instrument is fit for their particular purpose. The publishers of the Myers-Briggs assessment practise this openness, as do other high-quality examples of type measurement.

The type approach works in a coaching context: it is memorable, energising and focuses on the coachee – not on a theory, a process or the coach's expertise. This perhaps stems partly from the fact that it was not designed as a clinical tool. Some personality measures were initially designed to categorise and diagnose personality dysfunctions and still bear evidence of those origins. Type tools work best with people who are more verbally than numerically oriented; whose default model is win–win, not 'win at all costs' and who are reasonably self-knowing. But then again, such people seem more open to coaching in the first place. Far from the sort of stereotyping they are accused of, type measures are most effective in supplying a third voice which underpins conversations, the key contribution of assessment to coaching. A skilled practitioner will encourage dissent from the report as a core part of the coaching process. This is much more difficult with other instruments.

Type will appeal to coaches who prefer a top-down view of people: who take an overall view of someone's personality before examining the components. The next section looks at a contrasting approach.

Trait measures

As we have seen, type measures initially generate a simple notation of a person's personality: 'this person is an INFP' or a 'Research Investigator' or a

'Purple' or a 'triangle' or in whatever way different assessments structure and name their type system and its components. This top-level summary is memorable; that's one of its benefits. To go deeper you take it apart and look at the components that make up what can become, at its worst, a label. These components might be what the person suggested about a variety of actions and attitudes: their way of making decisions or what social situations energised or enervated them etc. Type sets off from the holistic, the integrated, then breaks it down: perhaps that's another reason the approach appeals to the human-centred coach.

Trait-based assessments approach personality from the opposite direction. They seek to identify the fundamental, simpler components of personality and build them up into an often subtle or complex profile which embodies this detail. The trait approach is often described as 'a-theoretical'. It tends not to start from any *a priori* assumptions, apart from some fundamental ones: that personality does exist; that it can be measured; and that it's made up of smaller components. Trait researchers gather and examine certain types of evidence, analyse it in certain ways and see what emerges.

What is a trait?

Trait is another word for a relatively stable and long-lasting personality characteristic. They help to explain why that person acts in a certain way. They can be contrasted with *states;* temporary feelings such as the elation you feel after your favourite sports team wins or the darkened mood when you miss your favourite TV programme by accident. States can be strong but they have a short half-life. Traits are relatively enduring. As we noted, personality expresses itself in different ways in different situations but, while the overall shape of a personality changes over time, this happens relatively sluggishly. It's therefore logical that many of its components/traits will move in the same way.

The word 'factor' will crop up often when you start looking at trait-based assessments in more detail. It seems to be a sort of synonym for trait. The test I use as an exemplar of the trait approach is called the 16pf® (which was originally known as the Sixteen Personality Factor Questionnaire, highlighting the factor-trait equivalence). A generally accepted and well-researched model of human personality is often known as the 'five-factor model' and many books refer to these sorts of tools as 'factor-based instruments'. The statistical method used on the raw evidence to identify personality traits is 'factor analysis'. I treat trait and factor as synonyms.

Trait-based assessments can be used for both coaching and development as well as selection to jobs. They allow for comparison between a person's personality profile and the different profiles of other people, a comparison which can be evaluated for accuracy.

Before looking at the characteristics of trait instruments in more detail, let me give you a specific example of how one trait tool was developed and the areas it uncovers. No trait instrument dominates the niche to the extent that the MBTI assessment dominates type. I've chosen 16pf to illustrate trait-based assessments. because I have used it and was also involved in publishing its UK adaptation for some years, working with some of the leading experts in its use. It was one of the first assessments to take the trait approach.

The 16pf®

Raymond Cattell and co-workers developed the 16pf during the 1940s. The tool has increasingly been used in occupational contexts to measure the personalities of employees and leaders but initially it was an attempt to research and describe the personality of human beings in general. It has applications in clinical and child settings as well as occupational areas.

Cattell applied a scientific, experimental approach to psychology; the 'lexical hypothesis' underlies his method. This suggests that significant differences between people are reflected in the language we use. Earlier researchers had extracted 18,000 words related to personality from major English language dictionaries then reduced them to a list of 4,500. This served as one of the starting points for developing the 16pf. The task was then to identify basic patterns within this huge list. Which terms were describing the same characteristic? Which clustered together? Which were entirely separate? Which groupings suggested a separate component of personality? Cattell and his co-workers studied three sorts of information: what went on in real life, for instance ratings people gave each other; questionnaire results; and the outcomes of laboratory experiments.

Factor analysis is the statistical method which allows you to provide correlations between and therefore find (or not) a structure in sets of variables. Correlations are reported on the news every day. One appeared yesterday as I was writing this: 'People who score high on narcissism are more likely to go into politics'. In other words, intercorrelation looks at issues like 'if this happens or occurs is it more or less likely that something else will or won't happen or occur'. If one person rates another highly on a particular trait, which we will call warmth, how likely is it that another person will rate them highly or that they will display what we have defined as warmth in their work or family behaviour?

Cattell correlated every variable with every other variable and formed a matrix, looking for underlying trends denoted by clusters of each variable, indicating that a factor (a discrete component of a whole personality) might exist. To make this a bit more specific, Cattell first took the initial word list and reduced synonyms and redundant words till there were 171 different trait names. He invited colleagues to rate 100 people on these 171 traits. By factor-analysing these results he found a smaller number of clusters. He then used questionnaires and research experiments to get ratings on this smaller group of clusters from a larger sample of people.

Factor analysis is central to how trait or factor measures are created and books like *Modern Psychometrics* (Rust et al. 2021) give more detail about it. Trait test users do not necessarily need to understand the fine detail of this sort of method, although they should understand what particular outcomes mean, so I have simplified this description.

If you looked at the 16pf technical manual, you'd realise that intercorrelating 16 factors is mind-bogglingly complex. Cattell and his colleagues undertook this analysis pre-computer, by hand; now they would use a specialist programme such as IBM SPSS Statistics or R.

What components of personality, based on the comprehensive word sample he started from, was Cattell able to identify? Examples include warmth, vigilance, perfectionism, tension. Another factor that emerged was reasoning, which came out as a major influence on personality. For this reason, the 16pf includes a short reasoning test but, partly because it is difficult to measure the full range of human reasoning ability with one short test, trait personality measures like the 15FQ+™ do not include a reasoning scale (hence the subtraction in the title!).

What sorts of questions does the 16pf ask and how do you answer? It tends to put forward everyday situations and suggest a way you might react. 'If my boss criticises me in front of others, I ask him to stop it' for instance. The person being assessed then chooses a response from a number of options such as:

Strongly disagree – Disagree – Neither agree nor disagree – Agree – Strongly agree

What's the output from a trait measure? Rather than the typical top-level type denotation of one kind or another (INFP etc.), trait reports tend to profile scores against the different factors.

Figure 5.4: Profile produced by an imaginary trait-based personality assessment

	1	2	3	4	5	6	7	8	9	10	
Aggressive			X								Passive
Wakeful							X				Sleepy
Creative				X							Conventional
Certain		x									Self-doubting
Romantic		x									Detached
Obsessive						X					Easy-Going
Materialistic								x			Idealistic
Self-serving					x						Other-driven

This is a profile from an imagined trait-based assessment to show what a profile might look like. X marks the score on each trait: the shading shows the range within which the true score is liable to sit. Different assessments will design these profiles in different ways. The report text then looks at how to interpret this profile. In some trait measures it will consider what each factor score means independently; in other measures interpretation can be subtle, looking at interactions between the different factors and how to interpret the shapes of the profile. Although at one time these reports became long, in recent years they have become shorter and have begun to use more infographics to reduce word count and reading age. Another trend has been that trait measures now produce many different reports for different purposes and with different readerships in mind – from trained users and business sponsors to the person taking the assessment. Some offer specific reports for coaches.

Because of their complexity, digitisation of the whole process of trait measurement removes a huge administrative burden; from the need to score results accurately and write out an interpretation, to the need to arrange assessment sessions in specific places. When used in development or coaching, assessors spend their time reading and understanding the report, discussing it with the assessment taker and then jointly developing action plans.

The 16pf illustrates some other points which are typical of trait measures. For instance, they usually give access to a manual which provides a lot of information about how the assessment was created, its history and its technical characteristics. Included in this will be a number of rather off-putting tables, which show the results of other groups of people assessed during the development or continued use of the measure.

Why trait measures differ

The number of trait-based tools can seem overwhelming. They differ, just as type instruments do. Some of these differences are particularly relevant to coaches. They are used in clinical, occupational and educational settings. Some trait-based measures, because of their perceived technical robustness are favoured in academic research: the NEO for instance is an example.

A key difference between trait-based personality measures is the number of factors they claim to be reporting on. So, as its title makes clear, the 16pf reports on 16 factors though its results can be looked at differently. This difference reflects several issues, one of which I have already mentioned: the fact that there is no certain, scientific definition of what personality is. Another is the status of the factors/traits themselves. Different experts suggest there are different species of factors or traits. Source traits (fundamental drivers of behaviour) and surface traits (ones which develop when those drivers actually express themselves in the world and are influenced by what goes on) is one such model. You'll find a similar one which discriminates primary and secondary factors. In some tests, primary factors are split up into what are commonly called facets.

Which is right and which is wrong: three scales, five scales or 57? There is no one objectively right answer for a coach: which test you use, measuring how many factors, depends less on trying to find the right answer to a scientific hypothesis than finding a model that you and your coachee feel comfortable with. The different numbers of factors in different tests offer you a choice so you don't have to fit your coaching hand into an abstract glove.

Ray Cattell exercised expert judgement in creating the 16pf. The 16 primary factors underlie the title of the assessment but if you further reduce these through factor analysis you get to five second order or global factors. Cattell wanted to balance usability with a genuinely detailed picture of the human personality and felt the five secondary factors were too coarse-grained to reflect the latter. As we will see, other people felt differently.

This is like setting the focus on a camera. Do you want to take a snapshot of all the guests to get an overall sense of the layout at the wedding reception; or focus on the couple's faces as an official wedding shot; or get a macro-shot of the central blossom in the bride's bouquet because you think it looks artistic? Do you want a rough picture of what's going on or do you want a much more detailed view which will take more time, make greater demands on interpretation but may be richer? Examples of the different numbers of factors in different titles include:

16 Factors: the 16pf measures 16 but you can take it down to five factors.

15 Factors: some assessments, based on the 16pf, remove the reasoning factor.

Five Factors: now the most common personality model, used in a huge number of assessments because of its technical robustness. In many of these assessments, the five factors are then broken down into many facets or sub-factors.

Three Factors: The 1975 Eysenck Personality Questionnaire measures three factors:

- E – Extraversion/Introversion
- N – Neuroticism/Stability
- P – Psychoticism/Socialisation

It is based on a view that personality is largely determined by physiology and genetics and, although it is technically impressive, is too narrow, too controversial and too clinically oriented to be of huge use to most coaches; although in recent years an adaptation of Eysenck's model has been applied in occupational settings.

One Factor: I attended a lecture on a one-factor model of personality in which one component explained everything. Or maybe I'm remembering an article in the much-missed *Journal of Polymorphous Perversity*®, now no longer published but once a type of *Mad* magazine for psychologists.

There are other ways in which trait-based assessments differ: the types of item format and rating schemes they use; the different ways in which scores are expressed and therefore analysed. What should be clear is that the range of trait measures will offer you one that fits your way of working and which reflects how you coach.

Examples of other sorts of trait-based personality measures

It's impossible to give an exhaustive list of trait measures. I have already mentioned a number and the field is fruitfully messy, including various applications of the trait approach I've seen used in coaching.

Peter Saville's assessments

There are other assessments that take a 'larger than three or five factor' approach. One example is provided by assessment suites developed by companies, SHL and Saville Consulting, founded by Peter Saville and his associates.

Saville sold both these companies but these assessments embody trends in personality testing over the last 30 years or so. Saville co-authored the Occupational Personality Questionnaire (OPQ) which was published in 1984 and later published Wave® with a company he founded in 2004. He is now heading up a third company.

Both the OPQ and Wave have been developed into a much wider suite of tools and reports since first publication. OPQ draws on the world of work and contributes hugely to leadership coaching. Its source is the 16pf but it replaced the language of psychology and research with everyday English and work-related concepts. Whereas the early versions of the 16pf, and other similar assessments, still exhibited traces of clinical usage in earlier editions, Saville's tests are focused on the working individual, teams and organisations. In this it charted the territory for innumerable work-focused assessments and the move to assessments which are shaped to address particular areas of life.

The OPQ also offers a range of different entry points at different levels of detail. The OPQ-32 has 32 dimensions but these can be looked at in four overall domains (relationship with people; thinking styles; feelings and emotions; and dynamism). Reflecting this flexibility, the OPQ also offers a range of reports driven from one assessment. Among others, it generates reports on teams, leadership, emotional intelligence, learning styles and ones linked to the publisher's own competency model. These reports have reflected and influenced changes in report format and design over the years. They've become less word heavy, more genuinely communicative and attractively designed.

In addition, OPQ offers different versions based on different measurement approaches. So there is a normative version, allowing you to compare a client with others and look at how strong a characteristic is; there is also an ipsative version, which allows the client to internally rank rather than rate characteristics and which makes answers more difficult to fake.

For coaches, the thinking style domain of the OPQ (comprising elements of forward thinking, detail consciousness, conscientiousness, rule following) is particularly helpful: it can suggest how a client will begin to solve problems and address issues. Equally, the Relationships with People domain suggests how the person will relate to the coach. The OPQ is by no means unique in this applicability but it gives an example of a specific area where assessments increasingly help. Eugene Burke's chapter on using the OPQ in coaching in the book by Passmore (2012: 8, 119–47) gives more advice.

In turn, Saville's Wave developed some of the ideas in the OPQ. It is partly driven by technological developments which allow it to offer users four different levels of complexity in its description of personality – from four clusters (thought, influence, adaptability and delivery) to 108 facets. The characteristics Wave exhibits are now seen in many assessments. These include the way technology is gradually virtualising assessments. Technological speed and capacity also allow the application of increasingly complex statistical techniques to data. This leads to assessments such as Wave which some – I include myself here – find over-complex. Others find it rich in its modelling of human characteristics.

Wave also reflects an increasing flexibility in assessments. There are tools that address one domain of human activity or category of person (young people, workers, leaders, sports team members) and specific aspects of those people (emotional intelligence of leaders for instance). But, at the same time, there are general assessments of personality which offer a huge variety of different reports, addressing different people and different aspects of these people. In some cases, the central assessment is the 'Intel inside' a huge range of satellite reports and conceptually related assessments, forming a sort of assessment system. This sort of system allows users to learn one assessment and then use this knowledge across a variety of applications – reducing costs and time taken to understand results at a deep and subtle level.

The bottom line is that you have much more choice as a coach as to which test best suits your needs, whether general or focused; detailed and complex or top level and easy to use; material or virtual.

Five-factor assessments

The five-factor model (often shortened to the FFM) is seen by many assessment experts as the standard: the best researched and most robust in its descriptions and predictions of personality. Increasingly, the FFM is ubiquitous. Cattell felt five factors were not enough to describe the subtleties of personality. So, in the 16pf, you start from the larger number of factors and then, if you want, can look at five more generalised global factors. Five-factor assessments are in some ways upside-down versions of this approach. They start with just five factors and then introduce a greater number of narrower facets. As a user, you need to decide which way up you want your pile of factors and facets to be!

You can argue for the first appearance of the FFM in practice as early as those five global factors in the 16pf or in the Pentagon Model in the original of the OPQ published in 1984.

The five factors are given different names in different assessments but the original list was:

- Openness to experience
- Conscientiousness
- Extraversion
- Agreeableness
- Neuroticism

Sometimes this model is referred to as OCEAN, after the initial letters of these factors.

Perhaps the best-known assessment of these, certainly the most academically examined, is the NEO instrument which measures the five factors and, in the NEO PI-R, six aspects of each of the five factors. The authors Costa and McCrae published the first edition in 1978. It has been revised regularly, and shorter versions have been produced. Fascinatingly, certain aspects of the model have even been found in non-human primates using the Hominid Personality Questionnaire. Developers have increasingly used the FFM as the basis of new assessments; as one tool within an assessment family which takes a particular approach; or as one report in the number generated by a particular assessment. Among its developments have been the adaptation of the model for different populations and uses. Some have been adapted for use in business settings. Facet5 is an example of an assessment using the FFM to address a number of issues in applied business psychology, not least coaching. The short form NEO has been used effectively with children.

The Neuroticism factor raises particular issues for FFM assessments and for other personality measures. The acceptability or otherwise of certain psychological words affects applied psychology in general and also assessment. One example of this is that organisational HR and leadership work began to accentuate positives rather than addressing weaknesses in developing staff. This has migrated into wider society as more people emphasise goal setting and the sense that 'you can do anything that you set your mind to'. The language of weaknesses and deficits has long been replaced by that of 'areas for development' and 'building on strengths'. The feedforward emphasis in coaching also emphasises the plus side. This issue is particularly stark when sharing the results of a five-factor assessment. 'Neuroticism' sounds like Freud's 'neurosis' and is interpreted by some people as a negative without ameliorating qualities. I know some recruiters who will simply debar someone from consideration for a job based on their neuroticism score.

> While attending a conference about a five-factor tool I, along with the other delegates, was asked to take part in an exercise based on our own profiles. A line was drawn on the floor. We were asked to stand on the line in a position that, in turn, reflected our score on each factor. Thus, if you scored 100 per cent on agreeableness, you placed yourself at the far-right end of the line: if 0 per cent at the extreme left end (although if that were your score, you would have probably argued with everyone else and been ostracised) and so on. This, by the way, is a technique for making profiles vivid, particularly in a team context. All went well for openness to experience, conscientiousness, extraversion and agreeableness – the usual mix of nodding heads, surprised expressions and energised questions and comments. When we lined up for neuroticism, however, there was a shuffling of feet, some worried looks and some reluctance to move anywhere on the line. When we sorted ourselves out, there was me and one other person up around 90 per cent and the rest of the course started giving us worried looks from the far end of the room: were we going to rant, rave or hallucinate?

The case study might suggest I am biased, but some of the most fascinating, and successful, people I have ever met have scored high on neuroticism. When tutoring advertising students at St Martin's College I discovered this was true of many of them. And I think it is no surprise that both I and the other person scoring high on that scale turned out to be coaches. In this context, neuroticism relates to how flexible you are in regulating your emotions rather than to pathology, and certain roles seem to attract people who score high on this factor. This example within five-factor assessments pinpoints why the use of any measurement tool in a coaching situation requires high-level communication skills, a sensitivity to verbal nuance and a genuine understanding of what a word, used technically, is meant to signify. Some assessment publishers have tried to solve this problem by using different words for neuroticism.

If you want to use a five-factor assessment, do look closely at how the neuroticism scale is dealt with and what language is used about it. Facet5 translates the Big 5 labels into simpler language: Will, Energy, Affection, Control and Emotionality. Its report specifically attempts to use value-free language and it looks at how emotionality, its equivalent of neuroticism, impacts on the other four factors. Other assessments have other ways of coping with these types of issues. Using 'emotionality,' 'emotional stability' or other alternatives may help.

Dark side measures

Coaches tend to be hired during times of change. We are sometimes brought in because someone feels their life or career has gone wrong; or because an employer or significant other thinks they are struggling. For instance, a lot of my recent work has involved working with successful, senior managers who criticise themselves for a failure to adapt effectively to board positions. The discomfort might be caused by their recent promotion; new owners; difficulty in communicating different sorts of information to investors rather than executive reports; a problem with work–life balance caused by job demands; or imposter syndrome.

As I write this, COVID-19 is complicating a VUCA world (one which is volatile, uncertain, complex and ambiguous). This puts huge stresses on people in all aspects of their life. In addition, we use psychological language more readily in description and explanation of everyday issues. On the day I am drafting this chapter, five headlines on one of the UK's major news sites use the term 'mental health' to explain the behaviour of well-known individuals or to highlight societal trends.

We have long known that there is no sharp dividing line between behaviour which seems normal and behaviour which suggests psychological distress or 'mental illness'. The factors that make up a personality are a continuum. So, the dark side model (and another approach known as the dark triad) applies itself to this liminal area where psychiatry and everyday life overlap.

The best-known measurement of this area is the Hogan Development Survey, published in 1997. It has 168 true/false statements which measure a wide range of factors, such as excitable, sceptical, cautious, reserved, diligent, dutiful. These are seen as possible blind spots leading to career derailment. I've used the Hogan Survey to begin to start discussing a cluster of questions, such as: 'Give me an example of what you do when the going gets tough. Is this appropriate? How do others react? Is it effective in making the going less tough? What behaviours do other people exhibit on such occasions? How would you react if other people acted the way you describe?' In doing this, I am looking at how someone's natural style might become counter-productive and damaging when it is used too much, or in too exaggerated a fashion in times of stress, worry and fear.

How is this different from someone whose behaviour may suggest that they have a psychiatric disorder? High-quality dark side measures distinguish personal style from personality disorder. Discussing dark side issues is not intended to diagnose but to consider how someone behaves, evaluating how much control they have over the behaviour, and how flexible they are in using different sorts of behaviour to get a required goal. Dark side measures are invaluable in helping certain sorts of people gain self-knowledge and start to think about controlling emotions and feelings, rather than being controlled by them. A chapter by Adrian Furnham in *Psychometric Testing: Critical Perspectives* (Cripps 2017) is an expert, readable introduction to the whole area, including the dark triad model of narcissism, Machiavellianism and psychopathy.

The concerns I raised about the factor of neuroticism (pages 62–63) are particularly pertinent here. You have to choose carefully who you use a dark side measure with and introduce it carefully. Even so, a number of the dark side reports are excellent and it is somewhat of a relief not to be using just self-congratulatory descriptions. With the right person, dark side reports can be rich sources of both agreement and disagreement, leading to genuinely enlightening discussions.

> Kieran is an entrepreneurial MD who is often brought in to revive an underperforming company. Each stage in his career has followed the same shape. He is invariably head-hunted. This reflects his charismatic personality, his ability to network and his high profile among his peers and in the press. During the honeymoon period in each role, he convinces shareholders and owners to give him new resources which enable him to grow the company quickly. He energises staff with dramatic in-person presentations and imaginative social events. Morale goes up. He asks for more new resources which threaten profitability but promise huge future returns. Progress slows and then meets increasing barriers to growth. It begins to miss its targets. Kieran is blasé about this and asks for more resources. More problems happen. Kieran gets yet more demanding and seems more excitable: he constantly addresses the staff of his company about the rosy future he is building – and begins to blame any problems on other directors and senior managers. Some are 'let go'. Before disaster strikes, Kieran is head-hunted again.
>
> In fact, this stresses the negative side to Kieran's stewardship. He is genuinely charismatic and entertaining. He does have strong strategic visions for his companies. He has a talent for financial analysis, but he applies it to other companies, particularly ones he is planning to buy, not to the one he is

running. And if he trusts someone, he trusts them without reserve, an unusual trait for such a leader.

Kieran was a difficult coachee until he was able to make his own choice of coach. Attempts to impose one (as he saw it) met with resistance. Once he had chosen a coach his immediate demand was to have evidence of where he could improve. Feedback gathered from his peers and his shareholders painted a mixed picture of his behaviour, identifying how his self-dramatisation ratcheted up as events spiralled out of control. Kieran nodded at this – he was not without some self-knowledge – but interpreted some of it as jealousy.

A dark side measure gave him pause for thought. The coach played up all the firms, companies and industry legends that had used it. This pedigree and the linkage with people he admired (or saw as competitors) was key to Kieran's accepting its findings to some extent. They painted Kieran as scoring high on 'emotionally uncontrolled', 'self-promoting' and 'dramatic.' The coach stressed that there was no sense in which Kieran could or should change his basic personality but a number of techniques were built on this to temper his tendency to lose control of himself when he should be controlling overall performance. Visualising techniques began to control his behaviour at critical points: he identified two or three people he trusted to take over certain tasks, including one he promoted to chief operations officer who took Kieran's ideas and actualised them. Stronger investment evaluation controls were brought in. And Kieran started promoting himself through carefully directed, edited and prepared online videos.

Kieran's career since then has had a similar 'boom and bust' shape: coaching couldn't completely change that. But the high and low points have been much less extreme and, arguably, there has been less collateral damage.

Factor-based assessments: pluses and minuses for coaching

Why should coaches use factor-based assessments more when type measures are already popular and regarded as effective in that context? They can seem over-complex in how they report their results, using often large profiles and their insistence on complex (though necessary) statistics. Type measures are more holistic, starting from a top-level description and offering the possibility of breaking this down if that is appropriate. Factor-based assessments tend to start from the factor (component) level and build up. It's easier to get a grasp of a type description than, say, become an expert in the many profiles you can get from the 16pf. The late Dr Wendy Lord wrote two wonderful books (now out-of-print) about interpreting a range of different 16pf profile patterns but these could not even touch the number that assessment can generate.

But too many people have taken type measures too often and can trot out their four-letter profile as easily as I was able to earlier on in this chapter. This can lead to distorted responses as the coachee fills in the measure 'yet again' and is influenced by their last set of results. Trait-based profiles are much less easily memorised and the way they are structured means it is less easy to trivialise or misunderstand them. It is much harder to manipulate the results of trait-based assessments: the sorts of questions they ask make it harder to give socially desirable answers or to guess which trait a particular question is addressing.

People take these sorts of assessments more rarely so there are fewer practice effects. Trait-based measures don't suffer the same technical criticism as type measures do. If carefully constructed, their results fit the normal curve of distribution. Five-factor measures are among the most researched and technically robust measures you can find. And, if coaching is only one out of a spectrum of services you offer, factor-based measures save you time and money since, having trained in them, you can use them for a variety of purposes. Type measures should not be used for recruitment: factor-based assessments can and are used for such decision-making as well as development/coaching discussions.

Factor-based assessments offer a different approach which will suit different coaches, coachees and coaching models. When you use any assessment too frequently it can lead to a degree of sloppiness in the coach because it all seems too familiar, so using a trait measure as well as a type assessment should ensure your skills are kept sharp.

Ipsative measures

The following section is slightly more technical and numbers-based than previous ones. I've taken this approach because the difference between ipsative and normative assessments is important for coaches and many people find it perplexing. As ever in psychometrics, the basic principle is simple once you get under the jargon.

Factor-based assessments allow you to compare responses to a norm group: the assessment results of a large number of people gathered during the development of an instrument. This allows you to compare different people's responses meaningfully – hence the use of factor-based instruments in areas such as recruitment. Let's say we were developing a normative personality assessment. *(The example here is purely to demonstrate the differences between two ways of assessing: it's not based on any existing assessment.)* The questionnaire might start like the one shown in Figure 5.5.

Each statement relates to a specific factor in the test – the first two might measure a factor I have titled 'Ability to influence'; the second 'Perfectionism'; the third 'Organisation'; the fourth 'Creativity'. If you score the first one 5, there are no constraints on how you score the others. You might say 5 for the first one, 4 for the second, 1 for the third, 5 for the fourth. The sum total of the scores anyone gives will differ from person to person: if there were 40 items in the questionnaire (ten for each of the four factors I've invented) the total score a candidate gave could potentially be 40 or 200, although either of these absolute scores might prompt you to ask a few questions about how someone was filling it in.

Figure 5.5: An item format for rating

For each statement indicate how accurately it describes you using the scale at the top where 1 is not accurate at all, 5 is completely accurate.					
	1	2	3	4	5
In meetings, my opinion usually carries the day					
No-one listens to me					
I like to deliver on my promises at work					
I never have enough time to do what I want					
I come up with completely original ideas					

Equally, two people might give their highest total scores to the ten statements measuring 'Ability to influence' but their scores on that factor might not be the same. Roger might score the first statement 5 and the second, which measures the same factor, 4. Rachel might score them both 3 and so on. Thus, even if they give 'Ability to influence' their top scores since this is most like them, you can see there can be subtle differences in the detail of your scores, allowing you to discriminate and compare differences. You can see not only that someone might view themselves as creative but you can see how they might differ from someone else who scores the creative factor high; you can also see how much more they consider themselves creative than the other factors.

What an assessment taker is doing when answering a normative instrument is **rating** their answers and rating one answer in a certain way still leaves us with total freedom to rate other items in any way we want within the design of the assessment.

By contrast, ipsative tools achieve a different description of someone by demanding a different style of answering: they ask you, in one way or another, to **rank** the areas you are trying to measure. The simplest ipsative measure might present you with the four dimensions I invented above and ask you to answer as shown in Figure 5.6.

Figure 5.6: An item format for ranking

Rank the following items 1–4 where 1 indicates your strongest quality of your 4 and 1 indicates your least strong quality	
Ability to Influence	
Perfectionism	
Organisation	
Creativity	

If you rank Creativity first among your strengths, you can't use that ranking for any other description. Two people might produce exactly the same ranking but they might be very different: one might see Creativity as overwhelmingly their greatest strength; another might see it as only slightly more of a strength than ability to influence. You cannot examine the differences in more detail and cannot compare the results based on the ipsative results alone.

Ipsative measures look at what's going on inside someone – how they rank their attributes, interests, motives etc. – not how their characteristics compare with those of other people. They often use a different format from the one I have outlined here, known as the forced choice format (see Figure 5.7). As its title suggests, this forces you to choose one answer rather than another. You will find this sort of format in some ipsative measures.

Figure 5.7: A forced choice assessment item

From each set of four activities, indicate which one you most like doing, which one you least like doing.			
Reading	Skydiving	Reading to the elderly	Baseball
Philosophising	Going to church	Bungee jumping	Doubles tennis

Over the course of the assessment with a number of these sets of four activities, the person filling it in is again ranking what he or she prefers doing. The specific options above would map onto a more general categorisation of interests: outdoor; individual; intellectual; spiritual etc.

Ipsative assessments: criticisms

One criticism is that you don't know what precisely a set of ipsative assessment measurements mean as compared with another set; for example, if you administer an ipsative assessment to Rory and Asha, and Rory has a higher score on a characteristic called 'Dominance', you will not know if Rory is very much or minimally more dominant than Asha. You can argue that ipsative measures are misnamed by the inclusion of words such as measure. An influential paper, 'Spuriouser and spuriouser: The use of ipsative personality tests' (Johnson et al. 1988) pointed this out in no uncertain terms.

Despite this criticism, ipsativity is probably the most common form of assessment used globally within work environments. This, in itself, raises certain doubts about the approach. Ipsative tests are often brilliantly packaged and marketed; some users, more even than is the case with some type tests, seem to become uncritical devotees rather than skilled and subtle users. Their marketing messages can make unfeasible claims. Over-simplification can lead to labelling people based on what they report in answer to 40 assessment items.

The other criticism levelled at these sorts of tests relates to the DISC system. This is a model of personality with only four scales known as Dominance, Influence, Steadiness and Conscientiousness, or some versions of these words. These personality factors stem from the idea that behaviour is influenced by two factors: whether you find the present environment favourable or unfavourable; and your sense that you are in control or lack control. This model underlies many popular ipsative personality tests. The criticisms of DISC have become associated with ipsativity and DISC can be criticised in lots of ways. The four scales seem closely interrelated and technical analysis of responses have suggested problems with seeing them as separate. These ideas and the model were propounded by William Moulton Marston in his book *The Emotions of Normal People* (1928) although it wasn't operationalised as an assessment till the 1950s. Marston was a lawyer, psychologist and creator of *Wonder Woman*. You can read more about him in *The Secret History of Wonder Woman* (Lepore 2018) or by watching *Professor Marston and the Wonder Woman*, a 2017 film. Controversy over Marston has been used, alongside technical criticisms, to damn DISC systems in some circles. But ipsative measures are not tied to his model although many use it. You can undertake other measurements than those based on the DISC personality model with ipsativity.

Why might coaches use ipsative measures if they are flawed?

First, ipsativity takes a within-person view of someone's personality, as opposed to a top-down, holistic (type) approach or a building-up-from-components (factor) approach. It can be used for a variety of different purposes, apart from unearthing personality and how someone might behave. If, for instance, you assess someone before they start learning a subject and then again when they've been working at it for a few months to see what progress they've made, you're comparing them with themselves. You're measuring ipsatively, and that measurement gives you genuine information which can inform decisions and action.

Whatever the flaws of ipsative tools, ranking is a natural and common human activity. It's a natural tendency to say 'I prefer this to that' or 'I influence behind the scenes rather than dominating a conversation' or 'I think Janet is a friendlier person than Sadiq', without always being precise about how much stronger one preference is than another or how different two people are. This sort of thinking is as important to us in making decisions as comparing and competing with others. It contributes to our implicit theories of personality which are so important to recognise and factor into the coaching relationship.

Put the above two points together and you can see that ipsative assessments avoid the comparison function that is central to some instruments developed in educational, clinical and industrial selection contexts and which does not necessarily suit coaching models and approaches.

Because they have been ostracised by many psychologists and academics, ipsative assessments have found a different niche from, say, those based on the five-factor model. This has resulted in many of them being easier and cheaper for users to get hold of. The dangers are beautifully produced, over-marketed, technically flawed products available with little or no training for little money ... or free. But it's ignoring real world concerns to underestimate how assessments that are available without long periods of training, and at a fraction of the costs of other assessments, will be immensely attractive to coaches, particularly those beginning to build up their coaching customers post-training.

Ipsative reports often use a simpler, everyday language than some others, avoiding the sort of technicality which makes reports difficult for coachees to understand or see as relevant to their own experience. Other sorts of tests are catching up here, and over-simplification can be both condescending and inaccurate, but many ipsative reports are immediately grasped by users. The trick then is to ensure that the Barnum effect is identified and called into question.

But there is one final, critical point. The 'Spuriouser and spuriouser' paper (Johnson et al. 1988) seemed to kick ipsativity into academic touch in the late 1980s. But the whole area of ipsativity has been re-examined and many of the technical criticisms have been challenged. Peter Saville (see pages 59–61) has been central to this re-evaluation. Saville's OPQ and Wave use ipsativity and he has been a major figure in arguing that both normative and ipsative measures have their different strengths. A summary of his arguments (and a discussion of what makes an assessment item effective) is in his jointly written contribution to *Psychometric Testing: Critical Perspectives* (Cripps 2017).

> Ipsative measures can be used to provide rich descriptions of coachees' characteristics. A colleague of mine was coaching Sandeep, a manager with a long, successful career in the food industry. A venture capitalist had bought the company Sandeep worked for and colleagues noted an immediate change in his behaviour: he seemed to be stressed and became very emotionally volatile under pressure. He fell out with members of his team, which was totally unlike him.
>
> My colleague was asked to coach him and after initial conversations used a tool from a family of assessments. This assessment uses ipsative-type questions but then presents the result as 'type' patterns. In addition, it looks at people in two ways: what someone feels is their natural way of operating as opposed to the way they need to operate in their present situation. There will always be some disparity but too much, for too long a time, can cause problems.
>
> This proved to be the case with Sandeep. Based on the results of the ipsative measure it was clear that he felt he was having to work a long way from his natural style. He naturally performed well where he had time and space to think things through carefully; he liked the accuracy of numbers and preferred situations which changed slowly or where some sort of status quo was maintained. The new owners were emphasising speed and change: getting results quickly by new methods. They encouraged competition and in response to

this Sandeep became super-competitive – hence the change his colleagues had noticed.

Sandeep 'got' the assessment results immediately and, in the next conversations, Sandeep realised that he was using a model of competition he'd learnt from his father, an aggressively competitive man. This led to practical discussion about techniques for responding to requests for quick answers and ways of interacting less competitively with his team.

Ipsative tests are often misused. but, as I think this case study shows, they can be helpful in coaching. They allow the coach and coachee to genuinely focus on the coachee's concerns and priorities, generating goals to which the coachee will be committed. However, if you are using them, be absolutely sure you know their limits and the technical quality of the version you are using.

Projective measures

There is one other approach to personality measurement, an example of which is one of the best-known assessments in the world, but which it is unlikely you will need to use. In certain countries, at least, this approach is hardly used at all; while in others it is popular. You may come across it wherever you live if you get more deeply interested in personality.

In the Rorschach test, originally developed in the 1920s, the subject is asked to look at a set of ink blots and explain what he or she sees. In other versions of projection, the stimulus material comprises scenes of people, a sentence to complete, elements to put together into a story. The stimulus material is 'ambiguous'; it is designed to resist a common interpretation of what it 'means' or 'what's going on' so an individual's response embodies aspects of their emotions, conflicts, personalities and ways of interpreting the world.

Projective tests originated in psychoanalytical thinking: they tap into unconscious drives which in turn fuel behaviour. Like ipsative measures, they focus on what is going on inside a unique individual rather than comparing a person with someone else. They are largely clinical in nature, often seeking to diagnose conditions such as schizophrenia or address relationship and familial dynamics. On this basis, projective techniques tend to look at aspects of the human personality which are beyond coaching's remit and a coach's competence.

It is difficult to mark projective tests objectively. Whereas the sorts of items I outlined earlier in this chapter can be scored, it is harder to affix scores to the responses you get from a set of ink blots, or a group of figures of indeterminate age and gender huddled under what might or might not be a tree. Projective measures are not classified as *objective* for this reason; to find out what the results might mean you need to look at the content of the person's responses and, often, need to learn a huge range of different responses from a veritable library of books. More recent versions of some of these tests have attempted to standardise their administration more and to provide scores from sample or norm groups against which you can compare one individual's responses to how other people responded. Some projective assessments, Rorschach for instance, have become slightly more objective in their measurement as they've developed.

Practically, learning to use these sorts of tests takes a long time. Interpreting them requires the application of high-level therapeutic expertise. It is unlikely you would want to use a projective measure in your coaching. But you might get asked about the 'ink blot test' by some of your more playful and informed coachees, or those who have watched TV series like *Frasier*.

Summary

These four basic ways of measuring – type, trait, ipsative, projective – can be applied to other human characteristics of personality: values, motivation and resilience, for instance. When considering personality, coaches will probably not need to use one of these species (projective) while type approaches are their overwhelmingly preferred choice.

There are huge numbers of different models of personality; some measure a lot or a few different objectively measurable elements, for many of which we can see physical/behavioural evidence; others are based on unconscious drives. There are also different options for how the coachee responds to assessment items to develop hypotheses about personality: rating, ranking and reacting are the three examples I have highlighted and there are more ways than I have had space to mention.

Underlying this variety, you will find a lot of commonality about the content of personality assessments, down to similar or identical items/questions appearing in different-looking instruments.

Despite the number of words used to criticise certain of these approaches, none is absolutely right or wrong, good or bad: there is no such product, despite advertising claims, as the best test for every purpose. Each approach is more or less appropriate and effective for a particular purpose. So, your choice of questionnaire depends on why you are using it and what you hope to achieve with it. It also depends on your comfort with a particular approach and the attitudes of your coachee. I would argue that it is best not to use a trait measure if someone is deeply cynical about psychology or if you find deeper statistical aspects of assessment difficult to grasp. But, equally, a type measure will be less than helpful if the coachee has taken the same tool 15 times and not been too impressed with the results.

Throughout this chapter I have suggested some approaches take what I have called a top-down, holistic approach; some build up from components; others concentrate on what the person in front of you ranks as most important within themselves. Your relative comfort and liking for these different approaches will tend to focus a lot of your usage in one area.

Figure 5.8: Different approaches to assessing personality

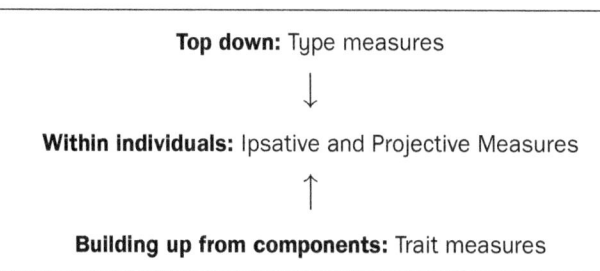

But it should be clear that there are many reasons for having more than one sort of personality assessment in your armoury, ranging from the over-use of the most popular ones to the sheer variety of purposes and differences between the people your coaching involves you with.

6 Assessing other characteristics

We bring many aspects of ourselves to bear on work, relationships and play beyond our abilities and our personalities. New types of assessment of these various psychological characteristics have increasingly been developed for business use, which is the most lucrative and largest market for assessment publishers and developers. Coaches working outside business market(s) need to decide how they will use these business-focused instruments. Do they need to use an assessment at all? If they do, is there one appropriate for a client addressing issues unrelated to their work? And if there is not, can an effective work-focused assessment be adapted for other contexts without distorting it? I will bear this issue in mind in this chapter as we look at some of the often-addressed areas of assessment beyond personality.

Emotional intelligence

Could the logical Mr Spock from the TV series *Star Trek* have evolved? The answer is a resounding no. Let us say a version of one of our distant ancestors – an unlikely Neolithic quantity surveyor – wanders along a hilltop track thinking about ordering materials from Wales for a new stone circle. She is suddenly aware of a strange sound she has not heard before. She stops walking and starts thinking through what it could possibly be: the invention of agriculture? Someone building a long barrow? A message from one of the gods? One of her tribe …? At which point the carnivorous beast which had been whetting its claws on nearby stones leaps on her and eats her. Later, our ancestor's sister – the emotionally aware one in the family – walks along the same path, hears the same noise, is terrified, runs like hell and survives.

Emotion short-circuits the time it takes to react to stimuli. By a pattern-matching process, we quickly identify a phenomenon as comforting, safe, strange, worrying, unusual, new or downright dangerous, and react accordingly and quickly. If we reacted purely logically, we would run through options serially, which would take a long time in which life-threatening events could happen. In the example given above, not only would there be one less Neolithic quantity surveyor, but the ancient British monument of Stonehenge would never have been built. Fear is an example of how emotion can, at times, help. It is invaluable in helping us survive and reproduce and therefore for our species to evolve. Disgust is another example of an emotion with survival value: it reduces our chance of eating rotting food, contracting dangerous diseases or hitching up with inappropriate mates who have careless – potentially dangerous – attitudes to personal hygiene. Our ability to short-circuit our rational reactions helps prevent what business thinkers name 'paralysis by analysis'.

Unfortunately, emotions can also lead us regularly to the wrong conclusions and the wrong actions: running away from what we think is a threat (but isn't); mistaking a threat for an opportunity and getting eaten. Sometimes emotion can overwhelm us, making it impossible to think properly, paralysing rather than energising us. Think about it for a while and you will soon come up with times when emotion helped you or hindered you: where appropriate anger has improved a situation; where an overwhelming fear has made you unable to say what you want – or even think coherently; when you mistook the emotions you were feeling. On other occasions, our inability to recognise and therefore react appropriately to *someone else's* emotions can lead us into trouble: a fight; causing hurt to someone we love; 'misreading the signs', blowing an opportunity at work or being optimistic about outcomes, based on our reading of others' reactions; not realising that not being told *not* to do something, for example, was actually an implicit suggestion that we were to do it.

Certain men typify all women as being 'too emotional' by virtue of their gender. That myth of feminine over-emotionalism still reinforces the glass ceiling in business and ignores the constructive part emotion can play in human life. Coaching with senior women executives usually touches on the effect of belittling attitudes and accusations of emotionalism by male colleagues.

To sum up, emotions are an important element in how human beings cope with the world. They can help achieve goals or form a blockage. They can affect relationships in and outside work.

What is emotional intelligence?

Formal definitions tend to state that emotions are 'strong feelings of varying length caused automatically by what's happening …'. But that does not offer much information and actually raises a number of questions and possible objections.

Evans (2019) suggests that while you might not be able to define emotions, most people know what they are. If asked the question, we would define emotions by giving examples rather than a form of words. He argues that the way we think of emotion has more recent roots than we tend to think: the word only appeared in book titles in the 19th century.

For some time, emotions were viewed as culturally determined and defined: different in different places. Recent anthropological research suggests that while indeed some emotions differ culturally, others are akin to a 'universal language': fear and disgust, are two examples of the latter. Such emotions are probably biologically determined.

Emotional intelligence (EI) is the skill at managing your own and other people's emotions; that includes identifying them correctly when they occur, understanding them and knowing what to do about them in different situations; the ability to use emotions, to control them rather than be overwhelmed by them. Another way of thinking about this is to consider a great writer who has an amazing skill with words: understanding what they mean and how to use them to communicate with different people in different ways. People with high EI achieve similar ends but their raw material is emotion.

The concept of EI appeared in 1964 but the first significant breakthrough came with Howard Gardner's 1984 book *Frames of Mind: The Theory of Multiple Intelligences*. Daniel Goleman's 1995 book, *Emotional Intelligence – Why it Can Matter More than IQ*, popularised work that had been done in the interim. It triggered huge interest in the area and its operationalisation in assessments, training courses and research efforts. This led to some claims being made for it. One formula I remember from the 1980s was that success at work was 40 per cent intelligence or IQ, 40 per cent EI and 20 per cent luck! I reckon that underestimates luck.

EI is a major element in an attempt to apply positive psychology. This built on the work of humanist psychologists, replacing an emphasis on illness, past problems and negative experiences with a stress on the positive; on achieving happiness and greatest possible achievement in the present and future. EI was, in particular, taken up in child and educational psychology. Many schools stress positive psychology and training in EI as part of their culture. EI has also proved popular in leadership coaching and training as leadership theory has come to emphasise the role of leaders in relationship building, communication and the motivation of colleagues, superiors and the people working for them, rather than the need for subject or technical proficiency.

Not only does EI help achieve goals and improve performance, but it also complements the concerns and roots of coaching. It is fundamentally humanist in conception and emphasises human relations as key to a fulfilled life. EI is a critical part of a coach's area of knowledge: being able to understand and control your own emotions to offer unlimited positive regard to a huge range of clients is an element in coach training; as is identifying, understanding and reacting appropriately to the emotions of the coachee.

But assessing EI is not without its pitfalls. I was involved in publishing one of the early EI assessments. The company I worked for wanted to start offering consultancy based round our instrument: we had no experience in this and, to gain it, offered a free service assessing and feeding back EI results to managers. One of our most experienced consultants and trainers went out to deliver the results of the assessment ... and came back some time later, shaking. The assessment taker had scored low on EI and, when informed of this, had grown monstrously angry and seemed to be about to throw our consultant out of the door shouting something along the lines of: 'I didn't get where I am today without incredible emotional intelligence'. The lesson being that most people (especially powerful men) are certain they have superior understanding of people and the people who don't have EI are the least likely to accept the judgement.

Assessing EI

Some online-delivered EI assessments– and there are lots of them – are free, require no training and can be self-administered with the report being sent directly to the person taking the assessment. Some of them are loss-leaders for consultancy, training, coaching and other forms of paid-for services. It is not so difficult to create a few items that look credible and interest people. Many magazines offer short assessments of these sort of issues: assessment as infotainment.

There are also many well-constructed online-delivered EI assessments. Two serve to illustrate the main approaches to the area and imply a third. Your choice of a tool will, to some extent, be guided by which one of these approaches convinces you. Put simply, EI is either a group of abilities or a subset of personality traits or a bit of both.

Emotional Intelligence as a type of ability

Figure 4.2 on page 39 shows the basic structure of abilities, dropping down from or building up to a general measure of intelligence or IQ. Each of these abilities (such as numerical and verbal) can be broken down to more focused ones. The diagram includes a box containing a question mark. Emotional intelligence may sit here, being a cluster of abilities, ones you can be more or less good at and, perhaps, learn.

The Mayer-Salovey-Caruso Emotional Intelligence Test (MSCEIT) is an example of an assessment which uses this model. It has four scales, basically about perceiving, using, understanding and managing emotions. These abilities are hierarchical; they grow as we mature. The focus of this tool is on how emotions affect thought and decision-making: improved EI leads to more productive thinking and decisions. MSCEIT doesn't just use standard multiple-choice items in measuring its topics, instead offering a variety of different item formats. There are, for instance, questions on recognising emotions that use pictures of faces, asking the test taker to indicate what emotion is being expressed, and pictures of places which focus on what emotions the pictures stir up in the viewer.

The authors suggest that even if you cannot learn certain aspects of EI, knowing where you score low can itself inform how you act. MSCEIT, like a lot of assessments, was originally developed as a clinical and research tool but there are plenty of others which take this ability approach.

Emotional intelligence as a personality trait

By contrast, the Trait Emotional Intelligence Questionnaire (TEIQue) is an example of an assessment which treats EI as a cluster of personality traits. In this case, the four are entitled well-being, self-control, emotionality and sociability. Each of these four factors breaks down into a number of more focused facets and there are also two independent facets. Over and above this sits a general score on EI: your EQ. These traits are measured through 153 items. This tool was packaged by the publisher for use in businesses and there are short forms for research as well as 360 forms for use with young people and children. The author is an acknowledged expert in the area and has undertaken a lot of research to back up his model and theories.

Some of the criticism of the whole idea of EI when it was first conceived was that it was not actually new or discrete from other human psychological characteristics that had been measured for many years: it was simply a repackaging. In one version of this criticism, it was argued that if EI was simply a subset of personality traits, you could get an EI profile from a standard personality test, and indeed that's what many personality tests now claim, offering EI reports as part of the range generated by a general personality test.

Both approaches

Goleman's original book defined EI in a way which drew on both models and there's no reason why an assessment cannot do that.

Can you coach EI?

My 'practice-based evidence' suggests that indeed there are areas where you can help someone to interact in a more emotionally intelligent way. In such cases, I work on simple techniques: breath control; specific ways of preparation for meetings and conversations; counting before responding; asking open questions; using triggers to more considered behaviour; using non-direction to buy time to think; visualisation. Many of my colleagues recommend practising mindfulness. The coachees often found this work helped them in other aspects of their lives – with partners, children, team mates etc.

Other intelligences

The book by Gardner (2006) on *Multiple Intelligences* proposes that there might be other sorts of ability or intelligence in the question mark square in Figure 4.2. Some might come up in specific forms of coaching. Kinaesthetic intelligence – the sort of physical abilities displayed by elite sportspeople – will be of interest to sports coaches as well as those involved in wider talent areas, such as dance. But multiple intelligence is a wider subject than we have space to deal with. In any case, their existence as separate characteristics is open to question. But such assessments are not that hard to find using key words in an online search.

Strengths

Many coaches use strength assessments. These fit well with positive psychology and coaching frameworks.

There are a number of approaches to this area, from coachees simply ranking a set of adjectives/nouns describing strengths, activities or roles, to fully norm-referenced assessments which ask the coachee to rate statements, then comparing their responses to others. You can identify a huge range of different strength assessments through a web search, similar in diversity to that for EQ: from infotainment quizzes to reasonably sophisticated, technically adequate assessments.

Some take an unusual approach. I tend to use StrengthsFinder, originally authored by Tom Rath (2007), and published by Gallup (Gallup 2007). In the version I use most, I buy the book which contains some background and more detailed descriptions of the 34 strengths that are rated. These are also referred to as talents and themes, and include titles like Achiever, Belief, Consistency, Self-Assurance, Strategic and WOO (Winning Others Over). Coachees tear open a pocket at the back of the book and this gives a one-use only access code to take the assessment online. This is a simple assessment, easy to use and reflecting directly what the coachee says: the report simply rank orders the 34 strengths with brief comments about what being strong in the area might involve.

There are more technically robust assessments of strengths recommended or referenced by other coaching experts. The Values in Action Inventory of Strengths (VIA-IS) was developed by Christopher Peterson and Martin Seligman, the latter of whom has become internationally famous for his work on positive psychology. It was published in 2004 and divides 24 strengths into six categories: Wisdom and Knowledge; Courage; Humanity; Justice; Temperance; Transcendence. This structure results from the researchers' attempt to provide a standard vocabulary to describe aspects of positive psychology. VIA was originally free online and technical information is light but there have been further developments of the instrument in more recent years (see www.viacharacter.org). Jenny Rogers discusses this assessment, and her use of it in a card format (Rogers 2019), but she also points out several of the difficulties of this whole approach. For instance, the names of strengths tend to be abstract and it takes time and some effort to relate them to the situation of a practically minded coachee or link them with concrete day-to-day action. This is not helped by the fact that some of the titles – see the examples I gave from StrengthsFinder – are opaque and need explanation and examples.

One of my problems with most strengths instruments – including StrengthsFinder – is the sheer number of strengths you sometimes have to deal with. It's difficult to focus and start meaningful discussions when faced with a ranking from the most to the least dominant of 34 strengths. You can try to agree that you will focus on a smaller number at one or the other end of the spectrum but there's a danger of ending up wondering if self-assurance is number 33 or number 29 on this week's strengths charts!

Finally, a lot of inventories of strengths focus on the work context. This means that some of the strengths that certain assessments deal with are specifically work-related rather than relating to what a coachee might exhibit in their particular situation. It seems highly likely that some common strengths contribute to becoming a priest, head-hunter, cricketer, parent, copywriter, poet and film star. But surely there will also be some strengths unique to a particular role and some, imperative to performing well in one area, which would be a weakness in another.

Assessment of strengths establishes a positive atmosphere and can win over reluctant coachees who would be suspicious of more heavy-duty psychological measurement. There is a danger of unthinking acquiescence to flattery ('Yes, of course, I'm strong in those areas which are the most important ones') and arguments about minute issues in the ordering of the ranking. I suspect there will be new developments in the assessment of the strengths area over the next few years, which will be of value to coaches and coachees.

Motivation, values, resilience and stress

I've treated these areas together for a reason; see Figure 6.1.

Figure 6.1: Motives, values, strengths and resilience

Motives, Values
Provide the fuel to set about what we want to do.

⬇

Stress
Internal and external obstacles to achieving what we want to do.

⬇

Resilience
Aspects of ourselves and our social environment which help us to overcome or recover from the obstacles to achieving what we want to do

These four human characteristics (motives, values, stress and resilience) are often treated separately in research and their definitions at times emphasise their differences rather than their connections. Yet they can be considered as a single system: two drive which goals you set yourself and how much energy you put into reaching them; one is a roadblock; one indicates how quickly you can get round barriers and resume your journey to your goal. There are assessments for these separate areas and, increasingly, linked assessments that look at the total process I have outlined.

Motives and values

The latest edition of an authoritative book on psychometrics (Rust et al. 2021) suggests that motives and values are similar. They certainly seem to serve a similar function. Motives energise and focus action. I sometimes describe values using a business term: a value is a 'red line'. If a value someone holds is crossed or denied, that person will react strongly – even violently. It's as though an enormous amount of energy is bound up in values: you only know it's there if the value is denied, otherwise it silently guides what a person does. Rust, Kosinski and Stillwell ask whether you can measure motivation when you don't know what a person values.

> Janaka was motivated in her job for a not-for-profit by seeing people recover from drug addiction to lead positive lives. Her values, which stemmed from Buddhist belief, included one that stressed the absolute need to support other human beings in difficult situations. An assessment or research paper might not use this sort of language in defining and naming a value: they will tend to use a more abstract noun, which creates the same problem of relating abstraction to the everyday which we noted in our discussion of strengths. Janaka was known as the calm centre in an organisation which dealt with tragedies, heightened emotions and distressing cases. She always came up with considered, reasonable, client-centred solutions to problems.
>
> The organisation that Janaka worked for was suffering severe financial difficulties and appointed a new business manager and CEO, both with business backgrounds. After some time, they seemed to be actuarially balancing cost savings against overdoses and deaths. Janaka, according to her colleagues, 'completely lost it'. She was unable to discuss strategic plans without losing her temper. Rather than suggesting solutions, she objected to suggestions made by others and, at times, insulted those people. It seemed to some colleagues that Janaka had suffered a nervous breakdown; to others she was an 'over-idealistic trouble-maker'. The new CEO suggested coaching which Janaka at first rejected but later accepted after a short holiday in which she discussed the issue with her partner.
>
> Janaka's values were so deeply embedded in her world view – as values are – that she found it difficult to discuss them and their effect on her behaviour. That's exactly why a values questionnaire and a measure of EI helped the coaching process. Janaka was interested in both areas and fascinated by the findings which gave her an explicit vocabulary, and a neutral external view, to discuss issues. It helped her understand that people have different values. It gave her the opportunity not to change her values, which would be difficult, even if it were an ethically acceptable solution to the problem, but to state what realising those values within the organisation might look like and how she might work to achieve this. This latter involved looking at her understanding of others' emotions, channelling her own without being overwhelmed by them and her spoken and written communication skills.
>
> She still disagreed with the direction the organisation was heading, and the values communicated by the new leaders, but she was now able to express her differing views with less emotional distortion.

These two characteristics – motives and values – seem to fit easily with coaching models. Any coaching relationship should include a discussion of whether the coachee actually has the will, energy, and interest to turn potential to actual, to set out to achieve an agreed goal. Other issues are important in ensuring this. For instance, lifestyle and health can hugely affect the energy to achieve goals (these are factors in stress which we'll also consider).

How might you measure motives and values?

Motives

There are many explanations of what motivation is and how it works; these in turn inform the different approaches that measurement takes. Few coaches, and hardly anyone interested in how people operate, will be ignorant of Abraham Maslow's Hierarchy of Needs. This is much criticised for having little research evidence to back it up and, in fact, for being plain wrong. It is also much distorted in the telling. But it does propose a set of hierarchical needs linked to motivation.

You may also have come across elements of Hertzberg's theory. Some factors motivate people: pay rises, job titles, innate job satisfaction, the feeling of doing good in the world. The absence of others can lead to demotivation – these are called *hygiene factors*, a term much used when I first became a manager.

Some motivators are external, such as pay rises, praise, other rewards, social contact. But you ignore internal motivators at your peril: achieving a difficult goal, the sense of a job well done, acting on deeply held values, meeting your own standards irrespective of what others think.

There is a temptation to think all people are motivated by the same rewards or outcomes, or by whatever motivates you, whether that is external material reward and recognition or an internal sense of satisfaction, achievement or value.

A typical, high-quality assessment of motivation at work is the Motivation Questionnaire published by SHL. This asks 144 questions which give scores for 18 motivation scales organised in four domains. These are:

- sources of energy such as power;
- where organisational culture increases motivation such as recognition;
- aspects of work people find motivating in themselves;
- external motivators such as rewards.

Individuals' results are compared with a norm group of others' responses.

By contrast, the Intrinsic Motivation Test from Getfeedback focuses on ten dimensions of intrinsic motivation, commenting that extrinsic motivations like salary can be dealt with during an interview or in a coaching session.

Edgar Schein's Career Anchors is particularly popular with some coaches specialising in work issues, particularly relating to career choice. It is a simple, easily accessible model available in book form. It is a self-assessment technique in which coachees investigate their career choices through investigation of their motives, values and competences, generating an anchor: the stable driver of a career. The basic findings can lead to rich, more detailed coaching sessions, looking particularly at career choice or if there is a mismatch between what coachees prefer in their work and the characteristics of their present role.

Many motivation assessments also measure someone's interests, since being interested in a subject or area of work will motivate someone to get involved with it. So, although we will look briefly at interests and their separate measurement, some motivation assessments cover the area.

Values

You can hardly enter large business receptions or go onto organisational websites without facing a statement of corporate values. These are often rarefied and abstract: what copywriters used to call mother statements – ones which no-one in their right minds would disagree with. Many are committee-written.

Some increase in the measurement of individual values stems from this corporate feeding frenzy. It's not unusual for HR and recruiting managers to talk about alignment of individual and corporate values when recruiting. They seem to mean that finding people who believe what the company says it believes will strengthen employee loyalty, encourage higher performance and increase valued employees' tenure. Values are also seen as key to other sorts of relationships; differences in the values held by members may cause conflict in marriages, partnerships, wider families and teams.

Because of this, among other influences, there has been an increased interest in values and their measurement. When I first became involved in assessment, the only two values questionnaires I knew had originally been published in 1967: the Surveys of Personal and Interpersonal Values by Leonard Gordon. They have been administered extensively in France and served as the basis for a popular careers guidance tool, among other applications. In particular, there's SOSIE: 2nd Generation™ published by Pearson Talent Lens (www.talentlens.com). This measures eight personality traits alongside the 12 values Gordon's assessments measure, seeking to address whether an individual's values match those of a team or organisation with a more accurate measure than is often used. These are: practical mindedness; achievement; variety; decisiveness; orderliness; global orientation; support; conformity; recognition; independence; benevolence; leadership.

Assessments influenced by the positive psychology movement tend to be less technically sophisticated. Some are just lists of questions with no underlying research. Different assessments take different approaches to naming, grouping and presenting values. For instance, some might classify values by what they relate to: family life, academic life, religion and spirituality. Others group them in more abstract ways: power, security, conformity. The simplest typologies divide values between the personal and the social. Different models will suit different uses and users.

The Values-based Indicator of Motivation (VbIM) positions itself in the space I mentioned earlier: matching employer and employee values. Its title links values and motivators in the way I've tried to, indicating that if your values match those of your organisation (or for that matter, relationship, family, culture, team) you will be motivated. It claims to factor in standard motivators as well as more contemporary and abstract ones, gathered together into four general areas:

- what I want for myself;
- what I want to become;
- what I want from others;
- what I want from society.

This 360-degree emphasis and linking of future wishes to present description is typical of the work of its publisher.

Stress

Stress is everywhere. It is the subject of radio and TV programmes, of articles in newspapers. It has occurred as side comment or subject in many of my recent coaching engagements.

This would not have been the case in earlier decades, certainly before the 1980s. You can 'factor' explanations for the ubiquity of stress to two general ones. The first is that stress is real and is caused by the rapid pace of fundamental change in society, a level we have not evolved to cope with. In particular, given the recent global pandemic, it is not surprising that human beings in many countries are experiencing hugely increased incidence of mild and major mental illness as well as stress. In short, our environment has changed and we are not adapted to it.

The second explanation suggests that, since the media, and health and policy experts have told us so many times that we're stressed, it is not surprising we feel that way. Being overworked, having trouble sleeping and other symptoms of stress have become a badge of virtue since the 1980s. The increased popularity of treatments for stress, such as mindfulness, meditation, retreats, breathing exercises and emphasis on diet and physical exercise, may have created a backwash in which more people feel they are stressed. However, as some writers argue, to suggest that stress is a unique contemporary problem is to ignore the lives of previous generations who experienced wars and medical treatments which sometimes sound worse than the illnesses, to name just two sorts of stressful experiences from an almost endless list.

I've seen stress defined by phrases like 'feeling overwhelmed' or 'being unable to cope with pressure'. Yet, like emotion, stress can have positive and negative effects. A little stress may actually improve your performance: if you don't feel slightly stressed just before you're about to play in a Championship game or run an online presentation with an audience of over 100 people or go on a first date, then you probably won't perform at your best. On the other hand, it's clear that experiencing too much stress over too long a period of time will not only damage your performance but also your physical health.

Because stress is so widely recognised as a workplace problem, it is an area where many organisations have created their own surveys and assessments. These are often designed to be filled in by a range of staff to identify those aspects of the working environment which are causing stress, often the hygiene factors named by Hertzberg. This further establishes the link between motives/values and stress that I suggested earlier.

In addition to employers' own assessments, there are also more formal tools available from publishers. StressScan was specifically developed with coaching and behaviour change in mind. It is organised into six areas: health, work; personal finances; family; social obligations; and world/environmental concerns. Unsurprisingly, the latter set of issues is becoming much more important: you will find many references to 'eco-anxiety' if you do a web trawl. One of StressScan's strengths is that it covers life issues beyond work. Coaches should look at the approach of any tool they are considering in the light of who they are coaching and for what purpose.

If this is a topic that emerges in the coaching process, spend time looking at the work of Sir Cary Cooper, the pioneer who single-handedly moved stress to the centre of public debate, health policy and organisational thinking in the UK. He developed what was the Occupational Stress Indicator, an early representative of the new generation of stress assessments. His many books cover stress in virtually every context in which it might occur. It is worth looking at the website of Robertson Cooper, the company he co-founded, which now describes itself as dealing with mental health, resilience and well-being.

Resilience

Resilience is a technical term from physics, indicating how quickly and easily a substance can return to its original shape or position after it has been strained in some way. It has come to be used metaphorically about people and, increasingly, about organisations, to indicate their ability to come back at least as strong as before after being knocked down or experiencing setbacks. In some cases, resilience is used to indicate the ability to keep performance, however you define that in different contexts, at a high level despite long-lasting pressure. No doubt by the time this book is published, there will be proposals to measure general national resilience after the COVID-19 pandemic

Resilience is an over used word but, in a world that is changing in ways which make Moore's Law look tardy, an increasingly critical one. Again, there are different approaches to assessing this issue. You can conceptualise resilience as a form of mental toughness. The Mental Toughness Questionnaire 48 (MTQ48) measures four independent scales which relate to this concept: control, challenge, commitment and confidence.

But the Robertson Cooper website mentioned earlier offers i-resilience on which you can measure your resilience through a free, 180-item questionnaire which looks at a wide range of issues that might affect resilience: Confidence; Social Support; Adaptability and Purposefulness. This is, in effect, a personality questionnaire generating conclusions about resilience. The site points out that while personality contributes to personal resilience, it cannot be the whole story and it asks questions outside the personality pool which illuminate an individual's work situation more generally.

Altogether now

Emotional intelligence can also be linked to this motives/values/stress/resilience model: lack of skill in understanding or managing emotions can lead to stress and also impact on our openness to accepting the social support that is so necessary for resilience at work and outside it. I have given examples of assessments which individually assess these different areas but, as the i-resilience example shows, personality assessment responses can generate insightful reports on an individual's resilience. Research also establishes a link between certain types of personality and susceptibility to stress. This ability to use one assessment to generate talking points about a variety of issues can save time, money and resources.

Another option is to use a linked set of tools which take the same approach. A recent example of this is flowprofiler® which, as its name suggests, draws on positive psychology thinking. It measures EI, resilience and motivation in one tool using one approach; or you can measure these areas separately with both teams and individuals. Alternatively, some companies –Team Focus is, at time of writing, an example – offer a range of tools for coaches and training in them through one unified course. They are EI and resilience scales and the VbIM. Team Focus's Type Mapping System, which I mentioned in the section on type approaches, suggests new developments in how we think about assessing human characteristics. Roy Childs, the company's founder, challenges preconceptions and ideas underlying some of the most established assessment approaches. He proposes that our views of personality are too static. He makes several distinctions: being and doing is one and he proposes that what someone does is not always what they are. His model suggests four selves: contextual; identity; ideal and unfinished. It models the way behaviour results from the interaction of external, environmental factors and our psychological make up. From this, he develops a detailed model of the non-sequential stages involved in generating behaviour. His thinking is influenced by Carl Jung and Will Schutz, the author of FIRO (see pages 94–95). It has implications for assessment of many areas; in these cases, he suggests more dynamic accounts which are less stable than traditional psychometrics has suggested.

Childs' thought is at times complex and will suit some approaches to coaching. His company is one of those that genuinely understands the needs of coaching and how that can influence assessment design. This is not the place to go into these issues in detail but if this kind of approach does interest you it is worth looking at the Team Focus website to get a flavour of their instruments' approach.

Other assessments are also beginning to deliver a range of results which provide a more nuanced picture of an individual, using different viewpoints and timescales. Some measure not only what you think you are like but how you would like to be viewed. Some stress assessments look at behaviours in different situations: when you are relaxed; when you are normally pressured and those which occur when you feel over-stretched. Techniques in these sorts of areas will change dramatically in the coming years, especially as we realise just how important our values are, and how contemporary living requires resilience more and more frequently.

Interests, learning styles and trainability

I have never had to use any assessments of these areas in my coaching practice, although I published and marketed several earlier in my career to schools and colleges and to what were then local authority careers guidance teams. They still tend to be used in educational environments (including, and up to, early career training and in colleges and universities) more than in adult coaching, although an interest inventory might occasionally crystallise thinking in the sort of career coaching Rogers discusses and sees as becoming more common (Rogers 2019).

Interests

Even if we are capable of doing a task, or learning a skill, we may have no interest in setting off for that goal or persevering at it. Interest inventories are used in career and educational guidance and stem from the work of Edward Strong at the Carnegie Institute of Technology in the 1920s. The Strong Interest Inventory® asks you to indicate your interest in several areas (jobs, leisure pastimes, school subjects etc.) on a three-point scale. A different ipsative approach is taken by some tests (the Kuder Preference Blank is an example) which ask you to indicate which activity they would prefer most and which least out of a set of three.

These sorts of tools are long; suffer boredom effects and the job role lists go out-of-date quickly. For instance, in my own lifetime, the job role 'secretary' has largely disappeared. Marketing roles have moved to focus on a particular area of applied digital technology, requiring sophisticated numeracy; the role required a range of characteristics, including verbal fluency, creativity and visualisation when I was a marketing professional. Interests are not necessarily long-lasting and are unrelated to ability. Just because you are interested in being a best-selling author doesn't mean that: a) you can actually write best-selling books or b) next week you won't want to be a research scientist. Nonetheless, interests are used in educational contexts with young people who have little knowledge of what certain activities entail, especially those who have, for whatever reason, not been given the knowledge, vocabulary and opportunity to make informed choices. That's why there are a huge number of these sorts of tools around. But my experience is that the best way to understand someone's interests, particularly people beyond school age, is to talk to them about these preferences and also to pick up enthusiasms through how people talk. Interests can be discussed in most general coaching without the use of formal assessment because the language used is non-technical and easily understood. Interests overlap; models categorising different sorts of interests are notoriously loose. Because of this, assessments of this area tend to be technically poor, offering different results on the same person at different times for instance.

Those involved in specialist coaching in schools and colleges will, in any case, know about key models and tools in this area, particularly those developed by John Holland at John Hopkins University. More recent tools developed in this context go slightly further than simply rating or ranking a list of types of interest. The Career Interests Inventory, for instance, asks questions about interests, competences and work styles.

Where someone is at sea during a process of job change, an interest tool might further their thinking and help coachees to articulate a want or move outside previous preferences. However, this has never been my experience and, if this is the case, you should examine tools to ensure the language is appropriate for your client.

Learning styles

My experience of assessing learning styles is similar: how people prefer to learn and learn most effectively is often easy to capture in conversation. People, particularly those with some experience of life and work, often volunteer that they 'don't have time to read', 'find out information from the net' or go on training courses. These sorts of comments can be queried: I've met only a few senior managers who have claimed to have the time to read books since 'being busy' is often a badge of virtue for this group. There are more robust models for how we learn than there are for interests. Kolb's model of learning styles looks at the interaction between concrete experience and abstract conceptualisation. Honey and Mumford, in perhaps the most widely used UK model, adapted Kolb's work and suggested four learning styles. Few education professionals, including coaches working in education, are ignorant of these models and the tools based on them. The Learning Styles Indicator, a more recent tool, relates learning style to Jung's psychological type. In turn this is linked to Kolb's influential experiential learning cycle. This latter moves through four stages: starting from a new experience, the learner reflects on it, develops an abstract idea related to it and then applies it to what they do. Linking and considering these models, the tool is intended to help people become more complete, flexible learners, not least in understanding that other people may learn in different ways.

It may be that older coachees, including those entering their third life, may be less aware of how they best learn and the various mediums for learning that are now available through new technology. However, learning styles tools have particular purchase in formal educational contexts.

Trainability

Similarly, trainability tests will rarely, if at all, be used by coaches; although the results of coaching might lead coachees on to training courses where trainability tests are used to predict likely outcomes. Trainability looks at how you think and process information and, again, some personality tests provide feedback on this area.

Conflict

Conflict, particularly between people and managers, is a core element in many of my coaching conversations. You can also see it in virtually every area of life from relationships within families to the way a team goes about playing a sport; from government success and failure to problems when a group of friends take a holiday together. At the centre of these phenomena is often a conflict between two people. Some people find conflict difficult to talk about. When they do talk, conflict often stirs up strong emotion which can become a hindrance in getting to the nub of the matter. Using an objective tool in such situations can help overcome these problems; the Thomas–Kilmann Conflict Mode Instrument (TKI® first published in 2001) is particularly popular. It requires no qualifying training or initial expertise because it is particularly easy to interpret, uses understandable everyday language and helps individuals understand how they handle conflict: from two basic dimensions, Assertiveness and Cooperativeness, to generate five conflict-handling modes (see Figure 6.2).

Figure 6.2: My version of the Thomas–Kilmann styles of handling conflict

ASSERTIVENESS ↑↓		
	COMPETING	COLLABORATING
	COMPROMISING	
	AVOIDING	ACCOMMODATING
	← COOPERATIVENESS →	

This simple accessible tool is supported by a wide range of other materials, from books to workshop materials, making it easy to trigger useful conversations around the issue.

> Anna's boss recommended coaching as a way of preparing her for promotion. 'She's a strong candidate', the boss said, 'but she lacks personal impact. In meetings she is often silent and I don't think she's firm enough with her staff. Performance problems tend to drift on and that's not good for the team – it will be demotivating for the people who are performing well.'
>
> The boss had been open about this feedback but Anna found it difficult to hear. 'I like to develop people,' she said. 'I believe in delegation and being positive not negative.' As far as meetings went, Anna was scornful about 'over-contributors who like the sound of their own voices'.
>
> Anna confessed that she had a dislike of conflict. She had grown up as the child of what she dubbed an 'overbearing' father and had protected herself by seeming compliant. Underneath her fear, she described disappointment and a wish to be more assertive, but somehow having lost the art of insisting on her own view.
>
> Anna's coach explained that the TKI took a generous view of all five of the styles it identifies, seeing a place for each of them, but that most of us can over-rely on one or two styles, underusing the others. Anna had high scores on Accommodating and Avoiding, a moderate score on Collaborating and minimal scores on Compromising and Competing.
>
> Anna came to see that while she did indeed have a talent for developing people, she was also over-delegating, leaving her staff exasperated and lacking guidance. She identified the typical occasions where the Competing style was necessary; for instance, in giving people corrective feedback or clarifying where the future direction of her team lay. The coach made the point that refusing to speak up at meetings was, as she herself said, leaving her with feelings of frustration – and the organisation without the benefit of her opinions.
>
> The coach's comment was that using the TKI gave Anna a swiftly understood and practical framework for understanding that conflict is a normal part of everyday life and that most of us have to work on developing expertise in using all five styles appropriately. This provided a fruitful platform for their work together.

In addition to looking at these core areas which may be coached, there are some techniques and instruments which can contribute to coaching in a particular way.

Repertory Grid Technique

Repertory Grid Technique is particularly suited to coaching: rather than imposing an external structure it enables coachees and others to choose and rate aspects of their life and work which enable them to construct and find meaning. This makes their priorities vivid and increases their sense of ownership of the process. It also reduces any coach bias in 'pushing' the coachee in a certain direction: this is genuinely a 'done with' rather than a 'done to' technique. The fact that it has not been adopted more widely is down to several factors: most importantly that it is not an off-the-shelf assessment you buy and apply; it's a technique you have to learn the use of which involves subtle human interaction, but it fits in easily in how coaching works.

The technique is based on George Kelly's Personal Construct Theory, developed in the 1950s. This suggests people use their own experience to develop ways of interpreting what goes on: he called these ways 'constructs'.

The topic of the coaching partnership is the starting point. This might be about any topic, such as starting dating again, buying a new car or changing jobs. Through discussion, the coachee establishes a set of elements for the topic. If the coaching topic was the fact that the coachee needs and wants to learn new skills, the elements might be the people who could facilitate this aim – an HR manager, their boss and others. Kelly suggested we make sense of these sorts of situations via constructs – based on past experience – which are always contrasts. So constructs in our example might be that these influencing individuals 'have access to training funds/have no funds'; 'are supportive of development/are hostile to development'; 'value my work/are critical of my work'. These constructs or schema are personal to particular coachees: they are the way they make sense of and find meaning in situations. There are a number of different ways of eliciting them described in Jankowicz (2004) and elsewhere. The way a coach elicits the basic topic, elements and constructs also maps directly onto coaching skills of open questioning, listening and challenging. Once these are all established, the coachee rates the elements against the constructs (how far the HR manager has access to training funds or not, for instance), resulting in a rich set of scores against topics the coachee has chosen, rather than one imposed on them by a particular assessment.

A training course or book will introduce this and how to interpret the ratings; it is then a question of practice. There are now computer systems for putting together the outcomes of the human interaction, which is the basis of this technique.

If you want to learn more about this technique, *The Easy Guide to Repertory Grids* (Jankowicz 2004) is an excellent introduction.

Team roles

We met in a centre which was used for rural team-building exercises – hikes, orienteering, building rafts and boats. The project was an unusual and exciting one. The participants had all paid a lot of money to be included in a round-the-world yacht race: most of them had barely been on as yacht before: some had never been on the water. The object of the workshop was to get them used to the paramount importance of teamwork in the dangerous environments they were going to experience. Well-placed trust could make the difference between life and death.

They had all taken the assessment which utilised team roles akin to the Belbin model, but they had not been fed back their results, nor had they yet been finally allocated to the crews that would take part in the race. However, they had been divided into teams by the organisers to complete a specific exercise – to make their way to a map reference on Dartmoor which was nearby.

The teams set off and, as was expected, several hours later rescue parties were sent out, found them and brought them back to the centre from various bogs, forests and tor tops. After a hot shower and a meal, the organisers convened a further meeting. The teams were fed back their individual assessment results but also the structure of each team. They were told their roles and that the teams had been specifically put together **not** to succeed, but to illuminate where lack of teamwork could lead to trouble. They discussed where their expeditions had gone wrong: in particular, often highly extrovert, success-focused male leaders ignored the more considered opinions of female thinkers, which led to teams taking the wrong course.

The next day, more balanced teams were put together; they were reminded of the issues from the day before and they set off for a different goal ... which they reached quickly with no need for rescue.

In retrospect, I'd question ethical/trust issues in the design of this exercise: deliberately leading people into trouble and potential danger will cause serious problems. But given what this was leading to – a round-the-world yacht race – this proved a powerful, transforming experience for the people involved. It was even impressive being a spectator.

Like the MBTI type system, Belbin Team Roles are easy to understand, provide a language that can be used to facilitate communication and is memorable. The Belbin company has more recently done a lot to build a range of products and services round the original model.

The model was created by Meredith Belbin over a number of years, in particular when he worked at the Administrative Staff College at Henley-on-Thames, UK. He and colleagues developed a game: when it was played, observers recorded different people's contributions and how they operated. This resulted in his 1981 book *Management Teams: Why They Succeed or Fail* and to the team role theory.

Team roles are, in effect, clusters of behavioural characteristics which contribute to team performance. They are informal roles, not like the job titles people are given or the particular task responsibilities people take on in a project or more enduring work team. The Belbin work roles suggest how people go about particular tasks and interactions. The roles Belbin suggests are:

- Resource Investigator: goes out and brings ideas back to the organisation to renew.

- Teamworker: gets the team to work together well.
- Co-ordinator: looks at how tasks are divided up, delegated and meet objectives.
- Plant: solves problems in unexpected and creative ways.
- Monitor Evaluator: is objective in weighing up priorities.
- Specialist: knows a lot about a particular – often technical – area.
- Shaper: have the drive to ensure team members produce work on time.
- Implementer: plans ahead and sees the plan gets actioned.
- Completer Finisher: ensures quality control of the finished product.

The Belbin company publishes a Self-Perception Inventory as well as an Observer Assessment which collects feedback from others (available from www.belbin.com). The process produces individual, team, working relationship, job and job comparison reports.

A way of making them vivid is to relate them to a team you are particularly interested in or know well. I use the Beatles – one of the most successful small teams that has ever existed as an example: John was the Plant; Ringo the Teamworker; Paul, the Shaper; George the Resource Investigator. When they were at their most successful, they had two other members: George Martin, their producer, was a Completer Finisher; their manager Brian Epstein the Co-ordinator. These are guesses but using this example I show the value of a balanced team – and the effects of losing one element in it without a replacement. Experience shows that a team of people sharing one or a very small number of roles will struggle; a team needs three or four differing roles to handle effectively the different issues it is bound to face

While these roles are used in team building, we know how understanding your own role, and learning to value the different roles of other people, is hugely valuable in individual coaching: highlighting strengths and preferences, and where best to use them in a variety of organisational and group structures. The Belbin structure facilitates discussions of conflict, suggesting that some roles are complementary and will naturally work well together. In other cases, coaching can address conflict, using team roles as a stimulus to discuss specific events. These roles are not unchangeable. We have a preferred role but also a number of others we can call upon if needed. If conflict between two people with the same role is causing problems, one of those people can make a team role sacrifice and begin to use some of the other behaviours.

In line with my overall argument, I think there are technical characteristics of this model which, though they might be criticised in other uses, are particularly suitable for coaching. Finding out your team role is both enjoyable and explanatory of day-by-day behaviours: it is simple to understand and memorable.

Other assessments generate team roles and/or focused team reports: most personality tests will provide some means of fitting individual profiles into a group or workflow structure. Types generated by type assessments are particularly amenable to this treatment. When I was involved in publishing it, the 16 Personality Factor Questionnaire explicitly generated Belbin team roles as it had been used in Belbin's original research.

The Team Management Profile is part of a range of tools published by TMS Development International. I used these a lot at one time since they combine the most communicative and energising concepts of type measures and the Belbin Team Role system and are focused on a realistic view of how a project or workflow operates through an organisation. They look at this from a number of different perspectives and provide individual and team reports.

FIRO-B®

FIRO-B® tends to get ignored by 'hard psychometricians' but used enthusiastically by some coaches. I could have treated it in the chapter on personality tests but, as the BPS review suggests, the FIRO-B is 'fairly unique among psychometric questionnaires in having this focus'. The focus this indicates is explicit in what FIRO stands for – fundamental interpersonal relations orientation. FIRO-B assumes that people are social animals and that our behaviour happens in the space between us. The tool is therefore not a comprehensive personality test but looks at how people work, act and live together. This is critical in work, family and team situations and recent world events have only highlighted the importance of social interaction and the dangers of losing it.

FIRO was created by an academic psychologist, Will Schutz, during his time in the US Navy in the Korean War: he studied teams running the combat information centres on surface ships and submarines. This pedigree explains in part why FIRO takes such a unique approach. Schutz later developed a more complex tool, Elements of Awareness, based on his FIRO-B work. This is still available but I will concentrate on FIRO-B here as the most readily available and widely used application of his approach in coaching.

FIRO-B builds round three areas: **Inclusion** is how much you want to be part of a group interaction you want with other people. **Control** suggests how much you want to be in charge of those interactions and your need for structure. **Affection** looks at the extent to which someone wants openness in their social interactions. The underlying thinking is as shown in Figure 6.3:

Figure 6.3: Underlying thinking of FIRO-B®

Everyone wants to some extent to feel	Significant	Competent	Likeable/loveable
Most of us have at least some fear that we will be	Excluded	Humiliated	Rejected
We will all have behavioural preferences about	Inclusion	Control	Affection

Because of the nature of what it is assessing, FIRO also allows someone to look at how they behave towards others and how others behave towards them, as well as looking at the differences between how these behaviours are viewed and how much they are actually wanted. Differences here fuel action.

Schutz's approach has not achieved the popularity of, say, those of Saville' or Myers and Briggs and part of the reason must be that, in business contexts, some people are suspicious of the words it uses: they sound a bit 'soft'. This has been somewhat rectified by the development of a business version of the instrument, which renames the categories Involvement, Influence and Connection. The interpretative guide to this was written by Judith Waterman and Jenny Rogers.

Using and training in FIRO also challenges the user; it demands a genuine emotional commitment. It has been argued that the only way you can get a true evaluation of the subtlety of FIRO-B is to go on a recognised training course, then to use it. It addresses fundamental human drives and its use demands human rather than technically mediated interaction.

360s

Most of the titles I've mentioned so far are primarily self-report: test takers give their own views of themselves. In coaching, this is, as I've tried to argue, a benefit. In some other decision-making processes, it is viewed as a weakness since it is prone to distortion, lying and self-blindness. In these latter contexts, 360s are sometimes viewed as more useful.

These 360s are designed to give you a more rounded view of a person. A set of items is presented not only to the person who is the focus of the assessment process but to a range of people who might know them, observe their behaviours and report on them. These will be different people in different contexts: family members; friends; reports, peers and managers in an organisation; manager, captain and colleagues in a sports team. When I managed salespeople, I would even ask customers to supply 360-feedback on how the salespeople behaved.

Nowadays, 360s are almost invariably delivered online. Organising, marking them and preparing reports by hand was a time-consuming and complex process in the days of printed questionnaires. Within a computerised environment, they come in a variety of different types.

Some self-report assessments are also available in 360 versions: other 360 assessments are based on competency frameworks offered by the publisher of the system. These usually enable users to choose which competences they want to assess. Others allow users to add their own items, either with the support of the 360 provider or, freely, in any way they want.

The most flexible environments allow you to set up questions you want to ask a range of people. Popular systems like SurveyMonkey allow you to do this.

How they operate

The coach sometimes decides who is going to fill in the 360 but, more usually, asks the person being assessed to nominate the other people. The process is then managed either by the 360 supplier or by the assessor using a web dashboard. Participants receive an email invitation, together with a deadline, and also get chase-up emails if that deadline is missed. Reports are generated automatically. It should include not only an analysis of the scores from different types of person but also provide free text comments.

Coaches can use 360s to add other voices to the conversation; to challenge the coachee; to encourage disagreement.

In looking to use a 360 from an external supplier, you should consider a number of points, not least whether the process ensures anonymity if it is needed. If the subject of the 360 has nominated the raters, they will probably know who answered in particular ways. The comment 'I know exactly who that response comes from' followed by an explanation of an incident that generated a particular view are commonplaces in 360 feedback – and for a coach are often gold dust, generating rich and challenging conversations, stories and questions. But sometimes anonymity is necessary for honesty.

Well-designed 360s leave a lot of room for free text comments. The design and usability of the report, how comfortable you feel interpreting it and sharing it, are important. As with any assessment, you should look at whether the assessment uses a vocabulary which reflects the area you are coaching in. You should check the number of respondents the system allows and whether it is available in a number of different languages if you coach internationally.

You can try out a new 360 to check on ease of customisation and of use; whether it can be used on different devices such as smartphones and controlled from a dashboard.

I use 360s in certain coaching situations but not in the way their designers intended. Experts in the use of such tools in work appraisal and other processes will comment on the care you need to take because ratings can be influenced by recent events and are consistently affected by the characteristics of the rater. For instance, women tend to rate themselves lower than male reports, managers and peers, while men consistently rate themselves higher; peers are consistently more accurate than any other category of rater in identifying issues in performance. The emphasis is on the ratings and I place little trust in their validity and reliability. Items used in 360 are rarely well-thought through and users can never be clear about where and in what state of mind people rated them. I find the ratings difficult to interpret; there's a danger of fixating on minor, meaningless differences between the views of different people. For the most part I find 360 reports, except in one respect, over-complicated, occasionally unclear and provide little useful information to inform coaching sessions. The exception is that I find some of the comments, the ones made with more care and attention, elicit stimulating reactions from 360 subjects. Often it seems that 360s supplied by outside companies are simply a way, perhaps over-engineered, to generate comments.

There is, however, another way of doing this.

DIY

Should you create your own assessments? If by that you mean, should you put together your own formal psychometrics to measure personality or motives, the simple, short answer is no, unless you're fascinated by the issue, are prepared for a lot of expensive, time-consuming training and have genuine statistical ability. There are too many effective assessments around for reasonable cost. Why reinvent the wheel?

But most coaches have, at some stage or another, put together a short set of informal questions which they have asked a coachee to answer in writing or during the course of a conversation. Getting informal feedback from colleagues, peers, significant others in this way – getting other voices to contribute to the conversation – can easily be done via just such an informal set of questions. Systems like SurveyMonkey can enable us to ask them online or, if it is possible, they can form the basis for a person-to-person survey as a coach gauges the feel of a company and the culture in which their client works. What you ask depends on the issue you are discussing but, in the past, I've used questions such as:

- 'Where does x excel?'
- 'Where does x need development?'
- 'What five words would you use to describe x?'
- 'Give me an example of a job where x excelled/x struggled?'
- 'What sort of role do you think x will take up?'
- 'Name five areas where x could improve; name me five areas where you think x will never excel'
- 'Where do you see x working in ten years' time?'
- 'Where would you like to see x spending more/less of their time?'

These questions can also be asked in a series of person-to-person interviews with others. But this can be time-consuming and difficult to organise. It also needs very specific skills to ensure the sessions are structured to give comparable results from different interviewees and to summarise these comments into a genuinely useful report.

There's an old parlour game I sometimes find useful in this context – though only if the culture of an organisation I'm working with is reasonably light-hearted. You ask someone to describe your coachee by comparing them to a series of common objects or well-known people. I use the format 'If this person were an x what x would they be?' where x can stand for a make of car, a rock star, a type of food or a colour. If people respond quickly, without second-guessing or examining the implications of what they say, you can get an unusually vivid picture of coachees, and one which draws on the creative side of their colleagues.

Getting teams involved in coaching sometimes suits DIY solutions, as long as you are clear that they are not designed for pinpoint accuracy but for rich incentives to talk.

7 'Is this assessment any good?' What the technical terms and numbers mean

Dragos had never worried about his weight much until his mirror told him that his lockdown diet was making him a new man – well, maybe a man and a half. He decided he had to lose weight. He bought a set of cheap scales then looked up what would be the optimum weight for a six-foot-tall man: different sources suggested a range between 140 and 183 pounds, which seemed imprecise. However, nothing ventured, nothing gained. He decided to aim for exactly 140 pounds.

Dragos weighed himself (for the first time in his adult life) and was horrified to see he was actually a 200-pound weakling! He couldn't believe this result, so he decided to check and discovered to his dismay that his weight had increased by two pounds in a minute. After another minute it had fallen four pounds. Over the next few days, he discovered that his second-hand scales measured his weight differently at different times of day. Dragos consulted the manual, checked and discovered they were calibrated to add a couple of ounces to his weight. He corrected them. They still seemed to deliver different measurements at different times. Two more sets of scales later (each more expensive than the last) and he was still getting inconsistent results.

Dragos's partner, Jean, suggested that she read the measures on the scales. 'Everyone lies about what they find when they weigh themselves ... I'll tell it like it is.' Dragos was lukewarm about this idea but agreed. After Jean had read off his weight to him and left the room, Dragos jumped on the scales again to check. The results were always different – sometimes higher, sometimes lower.

Still, over time, Dragos's weight went down. Finally, the reading on his now expensive scales was consistently under 140 pounds for a week, whether he or Jean checked. Dragos celebrated with a slap-up four-course meal for his whole family.

Later, he found other websites which gave different ideal weights for a six-foot-tall man (some were higher, some lower, some with a greater range, some a lesser). These were often related to age. He also found sites that suggested linking weight to height was not the best way to find out whether you were above or below average. Height to waist ratios and body fat percentages were two alternatives. Maybe he'd been measuring the wrong physical characteristic all the time. Dragos felt depressed and cracked open a fine bottle of red wine to improve his mood.

All measurements, including psychological assessment scores, have error built in. In Dragos's case I've implied some of the reasons that may be behind this, from personal bias to choosing a flawed measuring tool to not using a measuring tool at all. Dragos initially still had a vision of himself as a slim 15-year-old. But whatever you do to correct these sorts of issues, there will always be error. Psychometric testing textbooks tend to relate this to assessment scores through the equation:

Observed score = True score + Error

This equation applies to any measurement from your height and weight to the earth's distance from the sun and countless numbers quoted by politicians, journalists and social scientists. Too much certainty about a measurement is a besetting sin of many expressions of public and private opinion.

Like just about every other technical discipline, psychometrics has invented, and also co-opted, a range of technical and statistical methods to cope with this. They are designed to minimise naturally occurring error and get as close as possible to a true score of whatever an assessment is aiming to measure. As digital methods for data analysis have become the major means of looking at the accuracy of scores, techniques and technical vocabulary have reproduced at an alarming rate so, to many assessment users, the area has become even more opaque. Assessments look simple at first view – they're just a list of items or questions requiring responses. Look at an assessment manual however and, unless you have a specific cast of mind, you may lose the will to live. One of the reasons for this is that psychology tends to deal with areas that you cannot actually sense, that are internal. Measuring them requires fancy footwork.

Why is it important that the scores produced by assessments used in coaching are accurate? They're used to stimulate conversations, not to serve as the basis for life-changing decisions where accuracy is at a premium. In fact, the accuracy of assessment results and reports is still important in coaching in a number of ways. The credibility of the coach and the trust necessary for effective coaching would be damaged if a report were totally wrong or random. An accurate assessment will naturally contain error, as I tried to illustrate with the example of Dragos's lockdown weight, but a well-constructed assessment will minimise that error and show probable limits of that inaccuracy as well as how much you can trust the assessment scores. A carefully developed report will contain less than a purely subjective personal description of someone. Rather than chaos and misunderstanding, it will lead to rich containable disagreement.

What makes an assessment accurate is that it is objective, reliable and valid. In trying to find out if an assessment meets these criteria, it is important to bear two aspects of assessment in mind.

A lot of writing about these sorts of issues seems to be either by or for assessment constructors rather than assessment users. Assessment manuals too often read like the private conversations of a small, expert cabal. Much assessment training in the 1970s and 1980s had a similar bias. I remember not only trying to understand what a Standard Error of Measurements was, what it indicated and why it was important, but also having to learn how to work one out, by hand, on a data set. Assessment users will come across these sorts of terms in their work and they need to understand what they mean – they may indicate whether an instrument is designed for a particular purpose. But they don't initially have to learn how to work the equations out unless this helps the other understandings.

A second point is that, although this all seems complex, many of these techniques are simply reports of correlations (or dependence) which show whether there's a relationship, causal or not, between two variables. To give an example: it might be that the taller a person is the more interested they will be in football. One might be a partial cause of the other (the taller people may get enjoyment out of big sporting events because they can actually see over the heads of other people) or not. What a correlation shows is simply whether there's any relationship between the two things, not if one causes the other. The scores of correlations occur between 1 and -1.

1 = when one thing happens the other always happens
0 = there seems to be no relationship between the two things
-1 = when one thing happens the other never happens

You can work out correlations between more than two variables. Extreme scores of 1 and -1 are not to be expected; life is rarely that extreme, consistent or predictable.

Correlations underlie a lot of the data and how its accuracy is reported when developing a test. Here is a rough outline of this process.

1 Decide the overall area you want to measure.
2 How do you want to measure it? (For example: straightforward questions, scenarios, open ended answers, ambiguous pictures?)
3 Are there any sub-areas/dimensions?
4 Write/create items.
5 Get experts in the area you are going to be measuring to review the items.
6 Try them out on a sample of people.
7 Review. How are they performing? Are some measuring exactly the same characteristic? Are some not discriminating between different people? Do some seem to have nothing to do with the area you are trying to assess? (These are just some of the questions developers will ask.) Weed out non-performing items.
8 Gather data on the group you want to assess. Work out issues like reliabilities, validities etc. Set up predictive studies.

Bearing all these points in mind, let's now look at the sorts of evidence a developer might search for while going through this process, and you might look for when examining a test, to answer a number of critical questions.

What does this assessment claim to be measuring?

I was once involved in publishing and marketing assessments for schoolchildren. Some classroom assessments, which purported to measure numerical ability, in fact measured verbal ability as well: the instructions for completing the assessment were an unacknowledged test of reading and any child had to pass this before even understanding how to display addition and multiplication skills. This disadvantaged poor readers and those for whom the test language was not native. It happened that mathematically gifted children with poor language skills scored badly on an assessment on which they should have excelled.

It might sometimes seem obvious that an assessment is looking at motives or knowledge or stress. However, because these characteristics are elusive, what an assessment actually addresses might be something completely different.

Validity

Validity is the term used in psychometrics to indicate whether an assessment measures what it's supposed to measure. An assessment is valid if it does this. Validity can be defined in different ways: for instance, how correct the decisions and assumptions based on the results of an assessment actually are. It's also argued that validity is a function of a particular use of an assessment for a particular purpose: if you use an assessment to achieve a goal it was not designed for, and use it in a slapdash amateurish way, the results won't be valid; but used in a professional way for a different purpose the assessment might deliver valid results. But, for the moment, that first definition is good enough.

There are many different types of validity. One of the checks is to compare scores with other assessments. If a new assessment of, say, emotional intelligence (EI) scores relate positively to the scores on an assessment which has been proved to measure EI accurately, you have what is known as **convergent validity**. If the scores on your assessment don't relate in a significant way with assessments of other attributes, then you have **discriminant validity**.

One of the best ways to check the claims of an assessment is to leave it a while, then check if what it predicted comes true. So, if you use an assessment which predicts Sally will be an excellent salesperson, you can look at her performance six months or a year later and find out if the prediction was accurate. In this case you're looking at **predictive validity**. There are lots of other types; for example, does an assessment measure the whole of the area it is supposed to measure (**content validity**) for instance?

There is a type of validity which I think is of particular interest to coaches. One of the reasons why, for instance, the Rorschach ink blot test is not used widely in businesses in some countries is that most people will question what on earth these strange blots have to do with business. Rorschach lacks face validity in that environment. **Face validity** is the extent to which an assessment looks as though it's measuring what it is supposed to measure. To take the example of Sally, if you started measuring people's height and choosing salespeople on that basis, that assessment would have low face validity even if it predicted success at sales. As a matter of fact, I suspect height and sales success may be weakly correlated. If an assessment has low face validity it might well be that the person completing it treats it as a joke and the results are inaccurate. For coaches, using a test which seems irrelevant (even if, in fact, it's an accurate measure of a characteristic) will disrupt trust and suggest to the coachee that the coach may not know what he or she is talking about.

There are many other aspects of this question – new forms of validity – but hopefully this gives you an idea of some of the main ones.

Scores

There's a second, critical issue here. Sometimes we can score an area without knowing what the scores mean. Say Annabel gets eight out of ten answers right on her school maths test and Livingston only gets seven out of ten. Their **raw scores,** which is what we call them, suggest Annabel is better at maths than Livingston but we need to know a lot more about the questions before we can say that. For instance: how difficult were they? What order were they put in – hardest first, say or random? Was the test timed and had Livingston run out of time? Where were Livingston and Annabel when they completed the test? Did the questions use examples that drew on Annabel's experience or culture but not Livingston's? Unless we can answer those sorts of questions, we can't be sure which person is better at maths, nor what the difference between them actually is. To compare scores, you need to translate raw scores into standard scores where you know what the difference between two scores means.

So, norm-based assessments gather norm data which is the performance of a group of people from a relevant group during assessment development. Developers then work out the mean and the standard deviation, which is how widely the scores are dispersed about that mean or average. It's less important to understand how that's done than to see that this allows you to compare scores and be sure that the differences are meaningful. The score of anybody taking the assessment can be compared with that norm group and transformed into a standard score which will show you how much, for instance, someone is introvert or brilliant at maths or motivated by money as opposed to other people. So, to find out who is better at maths, you have to (among other things) convert Annabel's and Livingston's raw scores into standard scores.

In some reports, you see the scores imposed on bands such as **very high, high, average, low, very low** which are easier to understand. Standard scores come in all shapes and sizes. Percentiles are a common example. Someone who scores at the 50th percentile on, say, Neuroticism in a five-factor assessment is within the average range. Other examples are z-scores, t-scores, Stanine score which are simply different ways of reporting and comparing standard scores. Using assessments which report scores in these formats means you can begin to compare scores with others and see the relative strength of a score. Which norm group you compare the scores with – for instance, the general population, football managers, advertising executives, stand-up comedians – then becomes critical.

Does the assessment measure consistently and accurately?

If you measure something, you don't want irrelevant factors or the particular aspects of a situation to affect measurements. For instance, if you measured Moeen's personality on Monday and I administer the same test the next day you'd hope that any variation would reflect the error inherent in all measurement or a genuine change. There should not be variation owing to the fact that the administrations were on different days with different weather; one was in my office, one in yours; or that you and I administered the assessment in different ways because the instructions were unclear. The same is true for assessments delivered online: do you get the same results on an Apple machine or a pc or, for that matter, a Samsung phone? Are the results affected if someone completed the assessment in a hotel lobby as opposed to their home study?

As I've indicated, assessments used to be administered in quasi-laboratory conditions with detailed instructions in the manual to minimise irrelevant effects. Hence the term **standardised tests and assessments** which is still used today to denote the sorts of techniques we're discussing.

Reliable assessments are ones which measure consistently whoever is administering them: this is measured and reported as **inter-rater reliability**. Do you want to get different results if you administer the same test at different times? That depends, to some extent, on whether what you are testing for changes more or less quickly. Your mood may change hour by hour; your basic values will probably change little over a long period. So, **test–retest reliability** measures whether you do get the same results after a gap where results should stay much the same. Will your personality assessment results stay the same if you complete the same questionnaire after a gap of, say, a year or so? That depends on what you think personality is. If you keep giving someone the same assessment every month or so will the same results appear? Probably not: people can be over-tested on the same assessment, become used to it and be affected by practice or pay little attention to how they answer. This was a phenomenon I used to see on the UK graduate 'milk round' where students being considered for graduate level jobs were often endlessly tested on the same ability tests. It can be a problem for coaches due to the incredible popularity of the MBTI. You need to ask whether and how often someone has been assessed before you discuss yet another administration.

Developers will look at other issues to ensure an assessment is going to measure accurately and users can look at features of an assessment to evaluate it. For instance, **assessment items** need to be written in a certain way: so they should not include idioms, negatives, stereotypes or words that signify one or other answer. In a sense, test questions embody the sort of 'plain' style George Orwell proposed in his hugely influential essay *Politics and the English Language*.

Different ways of responding will be more or less effective in eliciting different kinds of information.

The **norm tables** included in a technical manual show the data gathered on different groups with whom an individual's score will be compared. It would be no use comparing someone's scores with a completely irrelevant group of people or a sample of two close personal friends of the developer. Examining the number of people an assessment was tried out on, how old the normative details are and how relevant the groups are to the purpose of the assessment is a way of getting a sense of how carefully and professionally it was constructed. Again, digital technology is changing procedures here. Whereas assessments were once revised and updated every ten years or so, digital administration means publishers can gather and make available up-to-date and new types of data quickly and easily.

To what extent can I rely on the scores?

Dragos's ideal weight, in the example at the beginning of this chapter, was between 140 and 183 pounds. He thought this looked a large range. Whether this was true or not, the fact that he was offered a range was a step forward from the usual media fixation on unwarranted accuracy.

The equation, *Observed Score = True score + Error*, indicates that we cannot be absolutely certain where the true score sits.

The **Standard Error of Measurement** for an assessment shows the margin of error you would expect in a test score and how confident you can be that the true score lies within a range. Some ranges are so huge as to make an assessment worthless: others give you a tighter banding which will prevent you making seemingly certain deductions from results which should prompt rich questioning.

In certain circumstances, going for a job is an example, assessment takers will be tempted to manipulate their responses to make themselves look good. This is less of a problem in areas such as development and coaching but even here there are times when someone will fill in an assessment in a way which does not reflect their true responses: out of boredom, especially with long tests; lack of interest; rebellion against the process they have been shoehorned into; a strong sense of humour. People can fill in a questionnaire randomly – to fit their idea of a 'successful' candidate or to stand out from the crowd; consistently agreeing with what they think the assessor wants. These effects all have technical names, and many excellently constructed assessments include measures of these strategies. They used to be called 'lie scales' but are now given more acceptable names such as 'social distortion' scales: they are measured using questions no-one could disagree with; the same question written in slightly different ways and other item types.

Some coaches might see this as running counter to the trusting relationship embodied in coaching. In my experience such information can, in fact, be a valuable topic of conversation ('Let's talk about whether you adapted how you answered these questions and why you think that was'; 'Tell me what you wanted to achieve by this').

Does it provide rich information in an economical way?

Assessments used to be long on the basis that short versions were inaccurate. Nowadays they tend to be only as long as they absolutely need to be, given most people's time poverty, shortened attention spans and inaccuracies caused by the boredom and fatigue consequent on concentrating on answering hundreds of questions.

So, both developers and users need to look at the time taken for administering, scoring, understanding, and feeding back an assessment and ask: is there a quicker, more efficient and potentially more insightful means of doing this with a different instrument or no instrument at all? While this is not strictly a technical point it is an important one, and one rarely touched on in discussions of tests.

Is an assessment fair?

There are cases where an assessment is illegal – where it intentionally discriminates against certain groups is one example. Another slightly different one is known as adverse impact where criteria are set which result in discrimination even if they are not intended to debar or work against certain genders, ethnic groups or whoever. The example often given is height requirements to apply for certain public service jobs, such as the police, resulting in fewer women getting jobs in those sectors.

But there is a much wider, contemporary issue which will affect assessment development and use for some time. Many assessments reflect binary views of gender in their language and data collection. They tend to assume that they are based on theories that apply globally. Because of this, it is rare that the basic approach of an assessment is adapted to reflect different cultures and their psychological insights. Recent research suggests this may be a mistake; there may be Chinese personality factors that do not exist in Western countries. Some assessments are based on a binary understanding of sexual orientation. Western cultural preconceptions dominate much psychology as they do coaching, which is definitely a Western construct.

Most areas of human activity are facing a similar challenge; assessment is no different. It reflects an understanding of certain issues before the rise of identity politics, the me-too movement, digital privacy concerns, the increased recognition of gay and other sexual orientations (in certain countries at least). These issues will affect both the language that assessments use, the sorts of data gathered and the definition of the norm groups with which an individual's scores are compared. As a simple for instance, if, as an expert in the area told me last week, there are 25–26 recognised, separate gender self-dentifications, how does this affect personal pronouns. Who does someone want to be compared with in an assessment context? This will be a critical issue in some forms of coaching soon; and will affect all forms of assessment. Watch this space!

What is an acceptable correlation?

That is a fundamental question. The fact is that experts disagree. Mike and Pam Smith (Smith and Smith 2005: 5) include a fascinating table which shows how well different criteria – from personality tests to age to years of experience – predict both success in jobs and in training courses. This table is old and is a meta-analysis of data over many different studies, jobs, training courses, assessments etc. But one of the conclusions is that, as we would have hoped, psychometrics are reasonable predictors in both areas, with correlation coefficients ranging from around 0.65 to 0.4 on jobs and 0.58 to 0.35 on training. Unsurprisingly, for reasons I have suggested, personality tests perform less well than, say, IQ tests. The Smith and Smith table reports a meta-data study of selection and has no direct relevance to coaching except to point out that no method of evaluating someone approaches anywhere close to a correlation coefficient of 1 – and a few, graphology and unstructured interviews for instance, approach 0. I have seen it written that a coefficient above 0.8 on any of these issues is encouraging and below 0.7 is not but that might be falling into the trap I mentioned earlier of claiming unwarranted accuracy.

Summary

In assessment training which genuinely prepares you for using a range of tools, you will go into these issues in much more detail. Hopefully, this chapter gives you a flavour of the area rather than trying to duplicate your course.

These issues might cause you to say, 'Do I need all this complexity?' My answer has to be, 'Yes, sometimes. And it's precisely the sorts of technical issues I'm signposting here that embody many of the benefits of using assessment.'

However much we have trained in coaching, however much we subscribe to the non-judgemental approach and commit to unconditional positive regard, our human judgements are continually diverted by our history, our experiences, our likes, our dislikes and our species' evolutionary history. Our judgements are often unfair and sometimes prejudiced and we are often not aware of these subjective biases. Coaches are (hopefully!) human beings first and foremost and are as subject to such influences as any other human being.

Assessments allow you to look at rich self- or third-party descriptions of someone you are coaching; understanding how the descriptions were arrived at and how much you can depend on them. You can compare their results with someone else and get a more accurate picture of whether someone is, say, introvert or as introvert as the next person. Assessments, in the best constructed cases, pre-empt unsupported dogmatism and open up a space for discussion. They are objective in that they are not swayed by prejudice.

8 The future

Assessment and testing are changing dramatically. Research will result in increasingly practical, available and affordable assessment methods different from those of the last hundred plus years. There are other engines driving these changes. Technological advance has been the main cause of innovation in just about every aspect of human life throughout history; we are living through the most all-pervasive example of this effect. Testing and assessment, like coaching, are not exempt. This is not least evidenced by the increasing use of technology to measure present human actions in order either to predict future behaviour or to effect behaviour change. We can see this in areas as diverse as governmental reactions to COVID-19 and the encouragement of vaccination to the sort of 'social scoring' that has been introduced in China. These examples raise psychological measurement as well as political and ethical issues.

Human demographics are changing. Living healthily for longer will change how people shape their lives: when they work for pay, when they study and when they enjoy leisure. But this is only one example of how demographic trends will influence human behaviour and therefore the extent to which psychologically related services and assessment might be needed. A rapidly changing environment and the slower rate at which humans as a species adapt is another strong influence.

Scanning technologies and other neuroscience-linked techniques are increasingly used to diagnose and uncover cognitive issues where tests and assessment were previously used. Treatment of strokes is a case in point.

The incidence of 'disasters' ranging from terrorist incidents to the pandemic to the inevitable effects of global warming affect how, where and how often assessment takes place. Mass migration and the growth in refugee numbers are likely to result in the need for more coaching and assessment focusing on topics as wide as cultural adaptation, educational choice, trauma, stress and work planning.

Assessment methodology, as that of any other discipline has progressed over the past 20 to 30 years. In particular, computing power and genuine research insights have offered different ways of delivering tests and interpreting them with greater accuracy.

Aspects of assessment that don't change or change less

The way we ensure that that data is valid and reliable, as dealt with in Chapter 7, will remain relatively unscathed (though they will evolve). Thus, even if you gather data using games-style items or people's Facebook pages, the statistical methods to analyse how accurate that information is will stay relatively stable.

Put simply: where you get data, then how you present it as information will change; how you check that you're not dealing in nonsense will, by contrast, change much less.

New sources of information

We still need psychometric assessments to generate data about people's psychological states. One prediction of the future is that soon we either won't need such tools or that they will be a much less important element in a wider mix.

Personal data is everywhere, nowhere more than on the internet and particularly on social media platforms like Facebook. In such environments, we are constantly making choices. Each **like** says something about our interests. Each preference fills in an area of our personality, as do the colours and designs we use to make, for instance, our websites more attractive. Looking at Facebook (and similar sites) we watch people making choices couched in their day-to-day lives rather than the artificial ones that assessments create. And, by the nature of digital technologies, all that data about human choices and preferences is organised, indexed, discoverable and open to interrogation. Michael Kosinski wrote his PhD on profiling personality in this way (Kosinski 2014) and the work in this area has developed further in recent years, as reported in the new edition of *Modern Psychometrics* (Rust et al. 2021). The most controversial use of this method was the Cambridge Analytica scandal. This continues to raise questions about privacy, influence and disclosure, not least in political strategies. Kosinski has repeatedly weighed the advantages of this method against attendant dangers.

In her chapter in *Emerging Conversations in Coaching and Coaching Psychology* (Watts and Florance 2021), Carol Braddick cites Alexa, Siri and other virtual AI assistants as other sources of information on which coaching can be based. They could use sophisticated analysis to hypothesise enduring psychological traits and temporary psychological states from the language people are using, the tone and speed of speech. Increasing sophistication in natural language production mean such assistants may also be able to generate assessment questions and coaching suggestions thus producing digitally mediated, spoken reports.

There are also beginning to be robust and proven correlations between physical states as measured by devices such as Fitbit and other wearables. This is not a new idea: biodata has long been an entry point for understanding someone else's (and one's own) mood. Pulse rate, sweating, increase or decrees in weight have always been data from which we extract psychological descriptions. The new wearables just make the process quicker, easier and, once more research has been done, more accurate. See Rob McHenry's chapter in the book by Cripps (2017) for an excellent introduction to this.

In a number of situations – airports, city centres in certain countries for instance – cameras are being used to record data which are then analysed by AI systems for a variety of purposes: to predict aberrant behaviour; to identify individuals who might pose a risk; to 'score' citizenship. There is no particular reason why this method should not be used for positive purposes such as providing coaching support to someone who exhibits the sign of a crisis. But since the introduction of CCTV simply to record what happens, this has been a hugely controversial area: one which is extremely specialist and which has been used for purposes which seem, to many people, invasive and undemocratic. As I write this, proposed legislation for the EU is seeking to limit the use of AI and put people first in a wide range of activities. It remains to be seen the extent to which its use in psychological services, including assessment, will be limited.

It is impossible to predict how many of these sorts of techniques will become practical and affordable and which will remain topics for fascinating research and even social and economic manipulation. It is certain that other sources – such as implants – will become more important and that the areas I have mentioned will continue to be developed. However, we are not able to predict how they will be regarded in the future and whether their use will be limited or made illegal.

In the context of coaching, these largely technology-driven ways of collecting the data presently elicited by asking questions may be a step too far. They may butt against the primarily humanist approach not only of coaching but of coaching and counselling psychology and certain ways of doing clinical psychology. But we would be wrong to ignore them. It is clear that certain of these techniques (wearables and digital assistants) do offer continual feedback. The issue is how these are used and the involvement of coaches in their development. At the very least, it's fascinating to watch the development of these technologies from a coaching perspective.

Transforming test items

Digital delivery and computing power have begun to offer new opportunities for the design of what can still be considered formal assessments and the format of questions/ items. For instance, rather than giving everyone who takes it exactly the same assessment/test we can measure the same psychological characteristic with different questions/items each time. There are several ways of doing this. For instance, let's say we want an assessment which measures exceptional numerical ability. Programmes do generate unique questions on the fly, based on a psychometric rule base, ensuring each version of the assessment measures exactly the same areas of numerical ability to the same level of difficulty. Or we can create a huge number of questions or items whose properties have been established (known as an 'item bank'), a unique selection of which is used in any particular testing session.

We can also shorten the time taken to assess someone on a particular characteristic. This can be done by a process known as 'adaptive testing'. We compare someone's responses on a few questions to how others have responded on those questions. This generates a hypothesis of the final results, which is refined and confirmed by a smaller number of specifically targeted questions.

These sorts of techniques have been around for a long time but have been made easier by computer administration and faster processing of responses.

Coachees who are used to DVDs, video games and the visually rich online will prefer more assessments which engage them more than printed multiple-choice questions, ink blots or geometrical matrices.

Gamification is the application of game-design elements and game principles in non-game contexts. Several companies are already promoting assessments influenced by this trend.

Like social media, games are psychological theatres. They require gamesters to choose, evaluate, show preferences, learn, predict the future, evidence ethics and react to change, as well as reason. They may even stimulate players to exhibit prejudices. These psychological responses are exhibited in sci-fi or horror scenarios and are used on magic swords and SS killing squads. New *serious* games apply them in more realistic, arguably relevant environments such as home, offices, building sites, power stations. With a sophisticated statistical underpinning and a focused design, tests can therefore be used to measure psychological qualities in an environment which seems more relevant to the test taker, leading to more accurate and engaged responses.

Just as assessment items are being influenced by technology, so are assessment reports. If test takers need to engage as they respond to assessment items, so assessment reports need to motivate and energise assessment users if they are to take on board their insights and, in coaching terms, accept the reports' insights as the basis for goal setting and action.

So, reports need to become visually richer. For instance, a film of someone acting in a way that suggests they score high on a preference for Introversion and low on Openness to Experience would be more engaging (and arguably, would be understood by more people more often) than a bar chart reporting percentile scores on those two personality scales.

Reports have traditionally been print-outs: why should they not become personalised websites, individualised podcasts or animated films edited to the particular needs of a test taker?

9 Conclusion

While I have been writing this book, my coaching sessions have taken place via Zoom, Microsoft Teams and other video conferencing programmes. At times I've been able to sit in on meetings distantly via online connections, enabling me to observe my coaching partners working in realistic situations. As we've grown used to them, web sessions have become richer. Different coachees and I have observed each other's body language, heard our tones of voice and speed of speaking. We have discussed and practised techniques: to my surprise an hour-long visualisation exercise based on presenting to a senior team seems to have worked well, despite the fact that the coachee was in Eastern Europe and I was in the UK.

All this acknowledged, there is an 'information deficit' in distant coaching as compared with in-person sessions. This has been partly made up by assessment results. If anything, my coachees and I have used them even more to create a shared language, encourage discussion, clarify issues and establish goals. Simple type and ipsative personality measures avoided misunderstanding and lengthy explanation. Strengths reports proved immensely face valid and engaging. Despite my criticisms, comments in 360 reports have proved immensely stimulating for conversation about healthy and disruptive relationships – both professional and private. Distant coaching is not going to go away and, in my experience, assessment contributes as much, if not more, in this context as it does in in-person coaching.

The downsides of assessment in coaching include some of the highly questionable claims to accuracy and comprehensiveness made for it; the way assessments tempt to simplicity and over-certainty; their somewhat authoritarian approach. Their upsides are that they provide rich information quickly; that it provides both quantitative and qualitative feedback which can be used in different ways; that the approach of assessment is adapting and will become more human-centred.

I have described how you can train to use assessments and I urge you to privilege instruments which do require training. These will be of a more professional quality. Good assessment training is more than a costly barrier to using measurement. In attending a well-constructed and delivered course you will be learning about what a good assessment measures – personality, motivation, a number of aspects of human psychology etc. – to complement your relationship-building coaching skills. Assessment training is stretching CPD for any coach.

I have mentioned many titles and it is worth starting your journey into the area identifying those types of instruments you need initially and those you put on one side to investigate later. My proposal is shown in Figure 9.1.

Figure 9.1: An assessment starter pack for coaches

Starter pack

1 At least **two** different personality assessments based on different approaches: probably one type measure and one factor-based tool
2 An emotional intelligence questionnaire
3 A strengths-based survey/questionnaire

Possible add-ons

1 Measures of motives, values, stress and resilience or one battery of assessments measuring all these
2 A 'dark side' questionnaire – if you are involved in executive coaching
3 A 360-degree questionnaire which gives emphasis to free text comments
4 FIRO-B®

Using these with skill and insight will contribute hugely to positive outcomes for your coachees and will give you an extra, enjoyable dimension to your coaching.

Writing this book has convinced me that coaching and assessment, far from being distant from each other or in conflict, are ideally suited to work together. Coaches approach their work in a way which, quite precisely, maximises the benefits of assessment and reduces potential negatives. The non-judgemental, genuinely power-balanced relationships that coach training helps us to create mean that we will use assessment results to increase understanding, encourage discussion and build actionable goals rather than to judge or categorise and leave the test taker wanting to know more.

Glossary

This glossary includes slightly more formal definitions of terms which are also defined in the chapters of this book, as well as terms which might be helpful in your investigation of assessment. These definitions are focused on the use of the term in coaching and assessment and ignore wider meanings (for instance in the case of words like 'factor' and 'profile').

APA: The American Psychological Association.

ATP: The Association of Test Publishers.

Assessments: Measurement tools of some aspect of psychology or behaviour (usually human). Can be distinguished from tests which are assessments made up of questions with right/wrong answers.

Dark side measures: measures of flexibility and inflexibility in individuals' behaviour.

EFPA: The European Federation of Psychologists' Associations.

ETPG: The European Test Publishers Group.

Factor: A dimension underlying a number of variables. In the context of this book, an underlying dimension of human personality.

FFM: the five-factor model of personality, sometimes known as the OCEAN model from the initials of its five factors: Openness to experience; Conscientiousness; Extraversion; Agreeableness; Neuroticism.

Forced choice: An assessment question which forces the assessment taker to choose their response from two alternatives.

Implicit theories of personality: theories we develop about ourselves and use, without necessarily being aware of them, every day.

Ipsative: an assessment in which the score of the respondent on one area necessarily reduces it on others. Scores on a particular area (such as a particular ability or a particular personality preference) in ipsative tests have to be considered in relation to other scores within the assessment rather than some absolute external criterion.

Item: The individual elements of an assessment that the person taking it has to respond to, including the possible response formats, including free-form

114 Glossary

writing, multiple-choice questions and different forms of rating, ranking etc. An item can be a simple question or can involve an ink blot, a diagram, a description of a situation and a number of other formats.

MBTI®: the Myers-Briggs Type Indicator, the most widely used assessment using the type model of personality.

Norm: An average score on an assessment, based on the performance of a standardisation sample.

Norm group(s): The results on an assessment with which the results of an individual can be compared. An assessment may have a large number of focused and general associated norm groups.

OCEAN: a five-factor model of personality. *See FFM.*

Percentiles: A distribution of scores can be divided into 100 equal groups: these are percentiles. Scoring on the 35th percentile means 35 per cent of scores fall below yours.

Profile: A graphic representation of the scores of an individual on different areas of an assessment: the range of factors in a multi-factor personality assessment, for instance.

Psychometrics: The area which measures mental states.

Raw scores: The basic responses of someone to an assessment. In a general knowledge test, it might comprise the number of questions answered correctly, the number of wrong answers and the number of questions unanswered.

Reliability: A measure of how dependable an assessment's results are, whatever the situation in which they are administered.

Standard scores: Also called a z-score. A score expressed as standard deviations of population scores with the mean set at zero. Most importantly, standard scores for different people can be meaningfully comparted with each other.

Stanines: A particular type of standardised score based on different criteria than percentiles.

States: Temporary feelings, such as the elation you feel after your favourite team wins or the darkened mood when you miss your favourite TV programme by accident. States can be strong but they have a short half-life.

Stens: A particular type of standardised score based on different criteria than percentiles.

Test: An assessment with right and wrong answers.

Traits: Distinct, reasonably long-lasting parts of someone's personality which help to explain why that person acts in a certain way.

Type: A classification of people. In assessment tending to be related to the type model originally propounded by Carl Jung.

Validity: A measure of whether an assessment assesses what it claims to assess.

Bibliography

American Psychiatric Association (2013) *Diagnostic and Statistical Manual of Mental Disorders – 5*, 5th edn. Washington: American Psychiatric Publishing.
Babiak, P. and Hare, R.D. (2019) *Snakes in Suits: Understanding and Surviving the Psychopaths in Your Office*, revised edn. New York: HarperBusiness.
Bentall, R. (2003) *Madness Explained: Psychosis and Human Nature*. London: Penguin Books.
Belbin, R.M. *Management Teams: Why They Succeed or Fail*. London: Heinemann.
Blauw, S. (2020) *The Number Bias: How Numbers Lead and Mislead Us*. London: Sceptre.
Bluckert, P. (2006) *Psychological Dimensions of Executive Coaching*. Maidenhead: Open University Press.
British Psychological Society (2020) *Guidelines: Psychological Assessment Undertaken Remotely*. Leicester: British Psychological Society.
British Psychological Society (2000) http://ptc.bps.org.uk/bps-qualifications-test-use. Retrieved June, 14, 2018., from http://ptc.bps.org.uk/.
Brock, V.G. (2014) *Sourcebook of Coaching History*, 2nd edn. Ventura, CA: Createspace.
Cattell, H. and Mean, A. (2008) The Sixteen Factor Personality Questionnaire (16PF), in G. Matthews and G.J. Boyle (eds), *The Sage Handbook of Personality Theory and Assessment Volume 2; Personality Measurement and Testing*, pp.135–58. London: Sage Publishing.
Chapman, T., Best, B. and van Casteren, P. (2003) *Executive Coaching: Exploding the Myths*. Basingstoke: Palgrave Macmillan.
Clance, P.R. and Imes, S.A. (1978) The impostor phenomenon in high achieving women: dynamics and therapeutic intervention, *Psychotherapy: Theory, Research & Practice*, 15 (3): 241–47. CiteSeerX 10.1.1.452.4294. doi:10.1037/h0086006.
Collins, M. (2018) *Beyond Imposter Syndrome*. Margaret Collins.
Cook, M. and Cripps, B. (2004) *Psychological Assessment in the Workplace: A Manager's Guide*. Chichester: John Wiley.
Corrie, S. (2020) Understanding, engaging with and generating research, in M. Watts, R. Bor and I. Florance (eds.), *The Trainee Coach Handbook*. London: Sage.
Cripps, B. (ed.) (2017) *Psychometric Testing: Critical Perspectives*. Chichester: John Wiley.
Evans, D. (2019) *Emotion: A Very Short Introduction*, 2nd edn. Oxford: Oxford University Press.
Florance, I. and Moyle, P. (2018) *Why Use Assessments in Coaching: Which ones? When?* Presentation, Berkeley Partnership, London, 15 May.
Furnham, A. (2017) Interview with the author on 'New Techniques in Assessment'. 5 May.
Gallup (2007) *StrengthsFinder 2.0 from Gallup*. London: Gallup Press.
Gardner, H.E. (2006) *Multiple Intelligences*. New York: Basic Books.
Gardner, H.E. (1993) *Frames of Mind: The Theory of Multiple Intelligences*, 2nd edn. London: Fontana Press.
Goleman, D. (2020) *Emotional Intelligence*, 25th Anniversary edition. London: Bloomsbury.
Gordon, A.M. (2020) In defence of Myers-Briggs. www.psychologytoday.com/blog/my-brothers-keeper/202002?in-defence-of-myers-briggs. Retrieved 14 February 2020.

Gratton, L. and Scott, A. (2016) *The Hundred Year Life*. London: Bloomsbury.
Groves, S. and Furnham, A. (2016) *Coaching as a Developmental Intervention in Organisations*. https://doi.org/10.1371/journal.pone.0159137.
Implicit Project (1998) *https://implicit.harvard.edu/implicit/*. Accessed 15 June 2018. Retrieved from https://implicit.harvard.edu/implicit/.
Jankowicz, D. (2004) *The Easy Guide to Repertory Grids*. Chichester: John Wiley.
Johnson, C.B., Wood, R. and Blinkhorn, S.F. (1988) Spuriouser and spuriouser: the use of ipsative personality tests, *Journal of Occupational Psychology*, 61: 153–62.
Jung, C. (2016) *Psychological Types*. London: Routledge.
Kline, N. (2002) *Time to Think: Listening to Ignite the Human Mind*. London: Cassell.
Knight, C. (2017) The history of psychometrics, in B. Cripp (ed.), *Psychometric Testing: Critical Perspectives*, pp.3–13. Chichester: Wiley Blackwell.
Kosinski, M. (2014) *Measurement and Prediction of Individual and Group Differences in the Digital Environment*. PhD Diss., Cambridge: Downing College.
Lee, G. (2003) *Leadership Coaching: From Personal Insight to Organisational Performance*. London: Chartered Institute of Personnel and Development.
Lepore, J. (2014) *The Secret History of Wonder Woman*. London: Scribe Publications.
Marston, W.M. (1928) *The Emotions of Normal People*. London: Kegan Paul, Trench, Trubner & Co. Ltd.
McDowell, A. (2012) Using feedback in coaching, in J. Passmore (ed.), *Psychometrics in Coaching: Using Psychological and Psychometric Tools for Development*. London. Kogan Page.
McDowell, A. (2016) The use of psychological assessments in coaching and coaching research, in T. Bachhirova (ed.), *The Sage Handbook of Coaching*. London: Sage.
McDowell, A. and Smewing, C. (2009) What assessments do coaches use in their practice and why? *The Coaching Psychologist* (5)2: 42–45.
McHenry, R. (2017) The future of psychometric testing, in B. Cripps (ed.), *Psychometric Testing: Critical Perspectives*, pp. 269–81. Chichester: Wiley Blackwell.
Mobbs, A.E.D. (2020) https://pubmed.ncbi.nlm.nih.gov/31961895/.
Moyle, P. (2020) Interview by author, London, 6 April.
Palmer, S. and Whybrow, A. (eds.) (2007) *Handbook of Coaching Psychology: A Guide for Practitioners*. Hove: Routledge.
Passmore, J. (ed.) (2012) *Psychometrics in Coaching: Using Psychological and Psychometric Tools for Development*. London: Kogan Page.
Peltier, B. (2010) *The Psychology of Executive Coaching: Theory and Application*, 2nd edn. Hove: Routledge.
Rath, T. (2007) *StrengthsFinder 2.0*. New York: Gallup.
Rogers, J. (2016) *Coaching Skills: The Definitive Guide to Being a Coach*, 4th edn. London: McGraw Hill Education.
Rogers, J. (2017) *Coaching with Personality Type: What Works*. London: McGraw Hill Education.
Rogers, J. (2019) *Coaching for Careers: A Practical Guide for Coaches*. London: McGraw Hill Education.
Roseveare, J. (2017) A practitioner's viewpoint: limitations and assumptions implicit in assessment, in B. Cripps (ed.) *Psychological Testing: Critical Perspectives*, pp. 251–62. Chichester: Wiley Blackwell.
Rust, J. and Golombok, S. (1999) *Modern Psychometrics: The Science of Psychological Assessment*, 2nd edn. London: Routledge.
Rust, J., Kosinski, M. and Stillwell, D. (2021) *Modern Psychometrics: The Science of Psychological Assessment*, 4th edn. London: Routledge.

Saville, P. and MacIver, R. (2017) A very good question, in B. Cripps (ed.) *Psychometrics Testing: Critical Perspectives,* pp. 29–42. Chichester: John Wiley.

Scoular, A. (2011) *Business Coaching.* Harlow: Prentice Hall Financial Times.

Smith, M. and Smith, P. (2005) *Testing People at Work: Competencies in Psychometric Testing.* Oxford: BPS Blackwell.

Stent, D. (2020) Interview by author, London, 16 April.

Stokes, J. (2020) Interview by author, 28 April.

Tiipins, N.T. and Adler, S. (eds.) (2011) *Technology Enhanced Assessment of Talent.* San Francisco, CA: Jossey-Bass.

Watts, M., Bor, R. and Florance, I. (eds.) (2020). *The Trainee Coach Handbook.* London: Sage.

Watts, M., Swinden, K., Al Khalil, C. and Cavett, E. (2020) The reflective trainee coach, in M. Watts, R. Bor and I. Florance (eds.) *The Trainee Coach Handbook.* London, Sage.

Watts, M. and Florance, I. (eds.) (2021) *Emerging Conversations in Coaching and Coaching Psychology.* London: Routledge.

Wildflower, L. (2013) *The Hidden History of Coaching.* Maidenhead: Open University Press.

Index

Page numbers in *italics* are figures.

16pf® 55–8, *57*, 65
360s 95–6, 111

ability tests 38, *39*
accuracy 103–4, 111
adaptations 33
adaptive testing 110
adequacy 31–2, 50–1, *50–1*
artificial intelligence (AI) 109
assessment 1–2, 40–1, *41*
   accuracy/consistency 103–4
   choosing 30–3
   contribution to coaching 2–9
   and economy of time 105
   fairness of 105
   feedback 25
   possible drawbacks 9–14
   preparation and administering 21–5
   questions for coachees 18–20
   questions from coachees 20–1
   research 25–6
   resulting measurements 99–106
   starter pack 111–12, *112*
   and tests 38–43, *39*
   when to use 15–18
   see also emotional intelligence; measurements; personality
Assistant Test User (qualification) 35
The Association for Coaching 28
Association of Test Publishers (ATP) 29–30

Barnum effect 11–12, 20
Belbin, Meredith
   Belbin Team Roles 92–3
   Management Teams 92
bimodal distribution 51, *51*, 54
biodata 108
Blauw, Sanne, *The Number Bias* 14
Braddick, Carol, *Emerging Conversations in Coaching and Coaching Psychology* 108
Briggs, Katherine 47, 52

Briggs Myers, Isabel 47, 52
British Psychological Society (BPS) 28–9
   assessment reviews 31
   Psychological Testing Centre 19, 22, 35–6

Career Anchors 82–3
Cattell, Raymond 56–7
change 8, 53
Childs, Roy 86
conflict 89–90, *89*
consistency of tests 103–4
Cooper, Sir Cary 85
correlations 56, 100, 106
Corrie, Sarah, *The Trainee Coach Handbook* 26
cost 33
COVID-19 63
culture 105

'dark side' assessments 24, 63–5
data
   protection 19, 21, 31, 105
   sources 108–9
delivery, assessment 32
difference, individual 6–8
disabilities 22
DISC system 69
discussion groups 28
DIY assessments 97

Elements of Awareness 94
emotional intelligence (EI) *39*, 74–8, 86
environment, assessment 22
error 13, 99–100, 104
ethics, and assessment results 19
Euro Test User Certificate 36
European Federation of Psychologists' Associations (EFPA) 29
European Mentoring and Coaching Council 28
European Test Publishers Group (ETPG) 29
Evans, D. 75

Extraversion (E) 47–8
Eysenck Personality Questionnaire 59

Facebook 108
factor/trait measures 54–66, *57*, *68*
fairness 105
feedback 25
Feeling (F) 48
fifteen factor model 59
FIRO-B® 94–5, *94*
five-factor model 55, 59, 61–3
flowprofiler® 86
Furnham, Adrian, *Psychometric Testing* 64

Galen 46
games 92, 97, 110
Gardner, Howard
  Frames of Mind 76
  Multiple Intelligences 39, 78
gender 105
Goleman, Daniel 78
  Emotional Intelligence 76
Gordon, Leonard 83
GROW 8

handwriting 20
Hertzberg's theory 82, 85
Hierarchy of Needs 82
Hippocrates 46
Hogan Development Survey 63–4
Holland, John 88
Honey and Mumford learning styles 88
humours 46
hygiene factors 82, 85

imposter syndrome 11
incompetence 11
intelligence tests 39
interests 83, 87–8, 108
The International Coach Federation 28
International Standard in testing 36
International Test Commission 29, 33
Intrinsic Motivation Test (Getfeedback) 82
Introversion (I) 47–8
Intuition (N) 48
ipsative measures 66–71, *67–8*

Judge Business School (Cambridge) 30
Judging (J) 48

Jung, Carl 51, 53, 86
  Psychological Types 47

Keirsey Temperament Sorter® 53
Kelly, George 91
kinaesthetic intelligence 78
Kolb's model of learning styles 88
Kosinski, M. 81, 108

language 5–6
  lexical hypothesis 56
Lavater, Johan 46
learning styles 88
Learning Styles Indicator 88
legislation, and assessment results 19
lexical hypothesis 56
Lord, Wendy 65
Lumina Spark 53–4

McDowell, Almuth, *Psychometrics in Coaching* 25
manuals 31–2
Marston, William Moulton 51
  The Emotions of Normal People 69
Maslow, Abraham 82
Mayer-Salovey-Caruso Emotional Intelligence Test (MSCEIT) 77
mental health 4, 13, 22, 24, 37, 38, 63, 84
The Mental Measurements Yearbook 29
Mental Toughness Questionnaire 4848 (MTQ48) 85
motivation 15–16
  motives and values 80–4, *80*
Motivation Questionnaire (SHL) 82
Myers-Briggs Type Indicator (MBTI) 12–13, 21, 27, 30, 44, 47–51, 52, 53, 54, 55

neuroticism 62–3, 64
norm groups 32

Occupational Personality Questionnaire (OPQ) 60, 70
Occupational Stress Indicator 85
one factor model 59
open access assessments 34
Orwell, George, *Politics and the English Language* 103
overinterpretation 12–14

Pearson Talent Lens 83
Perceiving (P) 48

Personal Construct Theory 91
personal data 105, 108
personality 5, 13–14, 33, 44, 72–3, *73*, 106
  defined 44–5, *46*
  and emotional intelligence 77–8
  ipsative measures 66–71, *67–8*
  projective measures 71–2
  serious problems 23–5
  trait measures 54–66, *57, 68*
  type measures 46–54, *46, 50–1*
  see also FIRO-B®
Peterson, Christopher 79
privacy 19, 31, 105, 108
progress 4
projective measures 71–2
psychological assessment 37–8
psychological evaluation 37, 43
psychological problems 23–5
psychologist associations 28–9

qualifications in assessment 35–6
questions, in the future 109–10

Rath, Tom 79
Repertory Grid Technique 90–1
research 25–6
resilience *80*, 85–6
restricted tests 37–8
returns on investment (ROIs) 8–9
Robertson Cooper 34, 85–6
Rogers, Jenny 38, 41, 51, 79, 95
  Coaching with Personality Type 47, 49, 53
Rorschach test 71, 72, 101
Rust, J. 81

Saville, Peter/Saville Consulting 59–61, 70
Schein, Edgar 82–3
Schutz, Will 86, 94–5
scores/scoring 32, 99, 102, 104
self-awareness 4
Seligman, Martin 79
Sensing (S) 48
Sixteen Personality Factor Questionnaire 55
Smith, Mike and Pam 106
SOSIE: 2nd Generation™ 83
Specialist in Test Use (qualification) 36
Standard Error of Measurement (SEM) 13, 104
starter pack, assessment 111–12, *112*

states 55
Stent, Dave 6
stereotyping 12–14
Stillwell, D. 81
Stokes, Anne, *The Trainee Coach Handbook* 19
strength assessment 78–80
StrengthsFinder 79
stress *80*, 84–5, 86–7
StressScan 85
Strong, Edward 87
Strong Interest Inventory® 87
Surveys of Personal and Interpersonal Values 83

Team Focus 86
Team Management Profile (TMS Development International) 94
team roles 91–4
technology, future 109–10
terminology/language 5–6
Test User (qualification) 35–6
tests 38–43, *39*
test–retest reliability 103
Thinking (T) 48
Thomas–Kilmann Conflict Mode Instrument (TKI®) 89–90, *89*
three factor model 59
trainability 88–9
training 31, 34–6, 99
Trait Emotional Intelligence Questionnaire (TEIQue) 77
trait measures 54–66, *57, 68*
translations 33
Type Mapping System 53, 86
type measures (personality) 46–54, *46, 50–1*, 65

validity 101–2
value-for-money 8–9
value-free distinction 43
values 80–2, *80*, 83–4
Values in Action Inventory of Strengths (VIA-IS) 79
Values-based Indicator of Motivation (VbIM) 84, 86

Waterman, Judith 95
Wave® 60–1, 70
Wildflower, Leni, *The Hidden History of Coaching* 43

www.ingramcontent.com/pod-product-compliance
Lightning Source LLC
Chambersburg PA
CBHW070239240426
43673CB00044B/1854